A Basic Course

in American Sign Language

TOM HUMPHRIES
CAROL PADDEN
TERRENCE J. O'ROURKE

ILLUSTRATED BY FRANK A. PAUL

SECOND EDITION

T·J·PUBLISHERS

This book was illustrated by the late FRANK ALLEN PAUL who pioneered innovative techniques for the illustration of sign language and established himself as the outstanding sign language illustrator in the country. Frank received his art training at the California State University, Northridge and at Otis and Chouinard Art Schools. Fluent in sign language, he worked as an interpreter but became a specialist in book design and illustration within the field of sign language publishing. He worked with Ursula Bellugi for a time as a research illustrator at the Salk Institute's Laboratory for Language and Cognitive Studies in La Jolla, California. Frank illustrated numerous publications including *A Basic Vocabulary: American Sign Language for Parents and Children* by Terrence J. O'Rourke, *Signs of Sexual Behavior* and *Signs of Drug Use* by James Woodward, *American Sign Language: A Look at Its History, Structure and Community* by Charlotte Baker and Carol Padden, all published by T. J. Publishers. Among other fine works, he illustrated *The Signs of Language* by Edward Klima and Ursula Bellugi published by Harvard University Press. Frank Allen Paul will always be remembered for his outstanding art and his dedication to excellence in sign language illustration.

Copyright 1994 T.J. Publishers, Inc. (Second Edition)

First Printing May 1994
Second Printing September 1994
Third Printing April 1995
Fourth Printing February 1996

Copyright 1980 T.J. Publishers, Inc. (First Edition)

Published by T.J. Publishers, Inc., 817 Silver Spring Ave., Silver Spring, MD 20910

Library of Congress Number 94-60050

ISBN 0-932666-43-4 Hardcover

ISBN 0-932666-42-6 Spiral

ACKNOWLEDGEMENTS

The efforts and support of many people went into the production of this book. We would like to thank the following for their ideas, criticisms, and suggestions on how to make this book useful for teachers of American Sign Language: Ben Bahan, Rubin Latz, Ella Mae Lentz, David McKee, Rick Rubin, and Darlene Scates. Also, thanks to Kerry Ancis for her editing which helped to improve the explanations and overall style of the book.

The models for our pictures deserve special thanks. They are: John Canady, Carlene Canady Pedersen, Joe Castronovo, Gil Eastman, Ella Mae Lentz, Dorothy Miles, Freda Norman, and Ken Pedersen. John Canady and Freda Norman, in addition to providing us with a breath of fresh air with their lively presences, were valuable consultants in preparing pictures for the sentences used in the text.

Ben Bahan, Carlene Canady Pedersen, and David McKee served as consultants on the sentences used in the explanations and exercises.

We also thank Cyndy Myers and Merrie Davidson for their patience and humor through a seemingly interminable process of typing, retyping and assembling the first drafts of the manuscript.

And for being a companion throughout all stages of bringing the manuscript to life, we are grateful to Frank Paul. As the illustrator and designer of this book, he constantly searched for and experimented with new and better ways to express our work in a printed form.

And finally, we are grateful for the moral support and encouragement we have received from our families, colleagues, and friends.

T.J.O.
T.H.
C.P.

SIGN LANGUAGE MODELS

| John Canady | Joe Castronovo | Gil Eastman | Ella Lentz |
| Dorothy Miles | Freda Norman | Carlene Pedersen | Ken Pedersen |

TABLE OF CONTENTS

INTRODUCTION

THE SECOND EDITION

In the years since this book was first published, there has continued to be a steady growing interest in the sign language used by Deaf people in the United States. An important factor in this interest is the ever growing body of research on sign language structure. These research studies have been of immense value in providing new facts about American Sign Language (ASL) and other foreign sign languages to hundreds of thousands of people, both Deaf and hearing. However, in order for the information from these studies to be helpful to the adult second language student, it must be in textbook form. This textbook, *A Basic Course in American Sign Language,* now in a new edition, incorporates the latest information about ASL structure as well as widely used second language teaching techniques and learning strategies.

This new edition of *A Basic Course in American Sign Language* retains the features which have over the years made it a bestselling ASL text. As before, the text is composed of 22 lessons. Within each lesson there are two to four basic explanations of the language structures to be learned. In each box there are examples and illustrations to explain the structure of the language. The basic format of *A Basic Course in American Sign Language* remains the same.

There are obvious problems with writing a textbook for a visual-gestural language. This text attempts to alleviate some of these problems by using illustrations and scripts for signed sequences. It should be clear, however, that attempting to learn a visual-gestural language from a textbook alone is no more advisable than attempting to learn a spoken language from a textbook alone. There is no substitute for a visual or spoken model of a language, and for this reason, this book is intended for use with a teacher or other visual models.

The following pages offer more information about how this book is structured and some considerations for its use.

DRILLS AND EXERCISES

The exercises are of several types commonly found in second language learning texts: substitution drills, transformation drills, and question-response drills. Substitution drills usually call for the student to substitute a single sign for another sign in a given sentence keeping the original sentence pattern. Transformation drills usually require a change from one sentence type to another sentence type (i.e., change a statement to a question). Question-response drills require the student to respond to a question asked by the teacher or another student. In all cases, the drills are to be signed, not written. The text is to be used only as a script for practice with the structures to be learned. Furthermore, no other language need be involved in any of the drills; practice is always in manipulating or changing one American Sign Language structure into another American Sign Language structure. Answers to the exercises are located in the Answer Key at the end of the text.

The teacher can develop additional exercises and activities where more practice in the structures is needed.

VOCABULARY

Many of the vocabulary items are included in the examples and exercises of the lessons. Although there are nearly 1,000 vocabulary items, the teacher may want to introduce other signs during the course of a lesson which are not included in the text.

The student should be aware that while one sign (for example, WHEN) is acceptable for one geographical region, a different sign is used in another region. We have included a few regional variations on some signs, but not all possible regional variations are included. The teacher may supplement the vocabulary sections with additional signs which are more appropriate to the local region.

The vocabulary sections are intended primarily for review purposes and the student should not attempt to learn any signs from an illustration without at some point seeing a model using the sign in some context.

DIALOGUES

In learning any language, conversational context is important. For this reason, several dialogues have been provided for this conversational practice. The dialogues are based on common situations found in the Deaf culture or within the deaf community. The student should first see the dialogues signed by the teacher or another sign model. The dialogues as they appear in the text should only be used as scripts (as with the exercises) to help the student memorize the lines in acting out the dialogues. In addition to providing a context and cultural insights, the dialogues can be used to develop a conversational articulation and fluency. Translations for the dialogues can also be found in the Answer Key.

GLOSSES (Writing system)

The sign

could just as well be represented in the text by ⊖, but since this would require that the student learn a new orthography in addition to learning a new language, we have

2

chosen to use capitalized English words to represent the sign translated as 'gas'. Note that the use of the English word, GAS, in capitalized letters is only a *symbol*. Do not be misled into thinking that the English use of the word, 'gas', is fully equivalent to the American Sign Language use of the sign GAS. As an example of the difference, the sign GAS is typically used for automobile or fuel gas, but not natural gas used in stoves or heaters—the fingerspelled sign #GAS is used for the latter.

The use of English to represent American Sign Language signs is simply a convention which we will adopt until a full writing system for American Sign Language is developed. The use of English symbols to transcribe American Sign Language sentences is intended as an aid to the student. These transcriptions or "scripts" are *not* English sentences.

The following conventions are used:

1. A capitalized word represents a single American Sign Language sign.
   Example: HAPPY

2. Several capitalized words joined together by hyphens represent a single American Sign Language sign.
   Example: DON'T-KNOW

3. Letters joined together by hyphens represent a fingerspelled word or abbreviation.
   Example: M-A-R-Y, T-T-Y
4. A capitalized word preceded by the symbol, #, represents a fingerspelled sign.
   Example: #JOB

5. The symbol, + +, indicates that the preceding sign is reduplicated.
   Example: TREE + +
6. The symbol, ~, between two signs indicates that the two signs are blended together in a smooth movement.
   Example: SEE ~NONE

7. The symbol, CL:, represents a classifier sign.
   Example: CL:F

A symbol such as CL:CC indicates that the classifier uses two hands.
Example: CL:CC

We have used some arbitrary characters with the classifier symbol. They are:
Arrows are used to show orientation of the palm or direction of movement of the sign.

•• is used to represent bent fingers.

° represents extended thumb.

↕↕ represents wiggling fingers.

TRANSLATIONS

Each American Sign Language sentence as it appears in the text or later in the Answer Key has an English translation. It should be noted that although one possible translation is given, this is not meant to imply that other translations are not possible. Translation from one language to another is dependent on many factors, not the least of which is context. In the absence of context, some translations in the text may be very limited in terms of the full potential of a sentence. The full range of possible translations should always be discussd with the teacher.

AMERICAN SIGN LANGUAGE AND ITS COMMUNITY

LANGUAGE, COMMUNITY AND CULTURE

Signing seems to arouse great curiosity in people who have little or no experience with it. The term "sign language" has traditionally been used as a generic term for different varieties of sign communication. But there is an important distinction between American Sign Language, also known as ASL, and other varieties of sign communication. ASL is a natural language. It is different in structure from the sign systems heavily influenced by English which go by different names: "Sign English," "Pidgin Sign English," "manually coded English," "sign supported speech," among others.

Exactly who uses ASL? American Sign Language is the language of a national community of Deaf people variously estimated to be between 200,000 and 500,000 individuals in the United States. A more precise number of Deaf users of ASL is difficult to establish because there has not been a recent census of Deaf people who use ASL. It is safe to say only that there are large numbers of ASL users in this country, probably more than speakers of French or Polish in the U.S. In addition, ASL is being learned as a second language by thousands of students who hear, in schools, colleges and other settings each year. It is entirely conceivable that within this century there will be as many second language users of ASL as there are first language users.

We have been capitalizing the word "Deaf" in this Introduction for a purpose. We use this capitalized form to refer to deaf people who make up local communities and a national community of ASL users. Why must a distinction be made? Because there are deaf people, who are not part of any of these communities, who do not know ASL. We are distinguishing between those deaf individuals who use ASL (Deaf individuals), and those who are deaf, but do not participate in the language or community of Deaf people, (deaf individuals). As you can see, just because one does not hear, it does not necessarily mean that one has learned ASL and is part of a Deaf community.

Conversely, there are also individuals who hear who use ASL and interact a great deal within Deaf communities. These hearing users of ASL are a part of the life of Deaf communities wherever they may be and they participate in the social and cultural life of these communities in many ways. They are, however, not Deaf. By learning ASL yourself, you too are beginning an exposure to a community and culture of Deaf people.

Local communities of Deaf people—east or west, north or south, urban or suburban, blue collar or white collar, African-American or White—all use ASL or some dialect or variety of ASL. Each of these Deaf communities has several basic things in common besides ASL: they have a history as a community that goes back for generations, they have defined systems of beliefs and patterns of behavior which have been passed down for generations, and they live within a society of people who hear.

These local communities comprise a large national community of Deaf people. Ask several people to explain what it means to be an American and you may get a different answer each time. So it is with Deaf Americans. Regional variation, class, ethnicity, race, and religion all are integral parts of this community of Deaf American Sign Language users. All of these communities and their local cultures contribute to what we think of as a Deaf culture in the United States. It is this culture of Deaf people from which ASL is generated and which has preserved and passed on its language from generation to generation for hundreds of years. There is a very large community of ASL users which is indicative of the power of a strong and vibrant culture of Deaf people persisting and thriving throughout many past generations to the present day.

COMMON MISUNDERSTANDINGS ABOUT ASL

It helps to understand what American Sign Language is by considering what it is not. Although ASL users gesture, as English uses sound, it is not merely gesture any more than English is merely sound. It is not mime. Even if you were an expert at mime, you would not be able to understand or use ASL unless you learned it first. This is an important point about ASL. It is not transparent, that is, one cannot understand it until one learns it. As with any language, it takes many years of study and interaction with people who use it, to be able to learn it properly.

ASL is not universal. American Sign Language users cannot understand Japanese Sign Language users, or even British Sign Language users unless they have first learned these languages. There is no universal signed language, just as there is no universal spoken language.

Furthermore, ASL is not derived from spoken English and has no roots in that language. Because of the various sign systems mentioned earlier that depend heavily on English structure, many people often get the impression that ASL is somehow a form of English simply made visible on the hands. This is not the case. ASL structure is different from English structure in some ways and alike in other ways. For example, ASL and English inflect for plurals in different ways, but they often use the same word order, as do many other spoken languages, such as French and Spanish. ASL also has grammatical features similar to some found in Russian and other languages.

ROOTS

Many languages have roots or influences from other languages. This is true of ASL as well. American Sign Language has existed in the United States since as early as the late 1700's. This country was colonized by various European cultures. In Europe, at that time, there existed several signed languages including French Sign Language and British Sign Language. We can therefore assume that signing communities of Deaf people in Europe had an influence on the lives of Deaf people in this country.

In 1817 a strong French Deaf influence was introduced in the United States through the establishment of a school for Deaf children by an American, Thomas Hopkins

Gallaudet and a Deaf Frenchman, Laurent Clerc. This historical event led to a process of convergence of two languages, American Sign Language and French Sign Language (FSL). (See Harlan Lane, *When the Mind Hears,* 1984, for an in-depth description of this event). As a result of language change over time, the American Sign Language that we know today has evolved into a language related to, but largely separate from French Sign Language. Someone who knows American Sign Language may recognize certain vocabulary and structures in FSL but not be able to converse in that language without learning it first.

The establishment of schools for deaf children also played another role. Prior to the establishment of residential schools for Deaf children, there was little record of large communities of Deaf people using ASL. Communities of signing Deaf people grew around these schools and in the larger cities beginning in the early and mid 1800's.

In the beginning, when the first schools were established, deaf children came from different sections of the country to attend these schools. It was not unusual for a boy from Georgia to be sent to Hartford, Connecticut to attend the American School for the Deaf. These children literally grew up in these schools because of distance and inadequate transportation at that time. After graduation, some students returned to their homes and many went on to become involved in the establishment of yet more schools. This process may have been partially responsible for the fact that, despite regional variation in American Sign Language today, there is enough standardization that the language is understood by Deaf people from all over the United States.

Even though spoken English was the primary language of the U.S. because of the large numbers of English colonists, there is little influence from British Sign Language found in American Sign Language. British Sign Language never seemed to get a foothold in the U.S., largely because of a lack of interest in British methods of teaching deaf children. Therefore, there were no opportunities for British signers and American signers to meet and exchange languages over a period of time. (John Van Cleve and Barry Crouch in *A Place of Their Own,* 1989 give a more in-depth account of the relationship between British and American efforts in education of deaf children.) Even the manual alphabet, called fingerspelling, which American Deaf people use to spell names and borrow English words, is the one-handed alphabet and not the two-handed alphabet used today by the British, Australians, New Zealanders, and Deaf peoples of other former British colonies.

THE CULTURE OF DEAF PEOPLE

ASL binds the American Deaf community but that is only part of the story. While the language is important to the maintenance of the culture, it is the culture that is responsible for the life of the language.

A few words about culture to help you understand the culture of Deaf people. We define a culture as a system of beliefs and activities by a group of individuals who are linked together by ethnicity, religion or language. One's culture underlies how individuals understand the world, their way of looking at things, their way of talking about things, their way of doing things, their system of beliefs, their plan to live by,

8

and their way of identifying themselves. Objects people use in their daily lives and how they interact with them are also culturally defined.

In the case of Deaf people, clearly their language and their common feature of not hearing link them together. You may observe cultural differences between yourself and Deaf people as you develop your fluency in ASL and interact with more and more Deaf people. This is a normal part of the process of learning a language. However, Deaf culture cannot be capsuled solely by the behavior of Deaf people that you see. You can only understand the culture of Deaf people by learning about very complex systems of meaning and belief that are the basis for Deaf people's everyday lives. Some of the behavior that you can see may give you insight into the culture, but it is important not to make assumptions about behavior you observe in Deaf people without understanding what generates that behavior.

PATTERNS OF TRANSMISSION

All cultures transmit their knowledge and beliefs to each succeeding generation. From one generation to the next, Deaf people have passed along their culture and language. However, there are several different pathways that a deaf person might take to becoming part of a Deaf community.

Some Deaf individuals learn ASL from birth from their Deaf parents and their parents' Deaf friends (and other Deaf children). They are exposed to their parents' culture from birth and this process is unremarkable in that it is much like the experience most people have who are born to a family that is American, French, Jewish, Southern, or of any other particular community.

For deaf children from hearing families, the most common pathway to a Deaf community is via other Deaf children in a residential school for Deaf children. Almost all of the states have a residential school which many Deaf children attend and spend a large part of their formative years. At these schools, the child encounters other children who are fluent in ASL and who are from Deaf families as well as, in many instances, Deaf adults who are teachers and houseparents. Through this interaction with other children and the Deaf adults at the schools, the deaf child learns ASL and becomes enculturated to ways of life shared by Deaf people. This pattern of transmission may also happen to a lesser degree in non-residential schools for deaf children where ASL is present.

Yet another pathway is through encounters between a deaf individual who has had no previous contact with ASL or a Deaf community, and someone from the Deaf community. For example, a deaf person could be born into a family that hears, does not use ASL, and has no opportunity for exposure to other Deaf children or adults. This person may not go to a school where there are any other Deaf children or adults. There may be no access to ASL or Deaf people in this person's environment until this person meets another Deaf person and this new friend provides an introduction to other Deaf ASL users. This is a very common process for many people who now consider themselves part of a culture of Deaf people. This process of enculturation, once begun, is long (several years) and requires sufficient intensity and frequency of contact to ensure the exposure that is needed for language fluency to develop.

BELIEFS AND WORLD VIEW

To be of the Deaf culture in the United States is to share with other Deaf people a complex system of beliefs about yourself, your community, ASL and the world around you. This intrinsic knowledge that Deaf people have allows them to generate behaviors, know and interpret the world, and go about their daily lives in particular ways that we see and remark upon as being "Deaf."

A good place to look for a clue to the way Deaf people see themselves is in the group's official term used for themselves: DEAF (capitalization is used to indicate an ASL sign). In contrast, the term "hearing impaired" is seldom used in reference to the group or to group identity but rather is used when talking about other institutions involving hearing people, such as schools for the hearing impaired and organizations of mostly hearing people.

What is interesting is that among Deaf people, the signs DEAF and HARD-OF-HEARING do not necessarily refer to degrees of hearing but rather to a perception of oneself or of another person who does not hear. DEAF marks a central connection to the group while HARD-OF-HEARING marks another kind of identity, meaning those who display characteristics of hearing people such as speaking, using the telephone and other hearing-like behaviors.

These labels are cultural rather than strictly audiological. There are DEAF people who hear to some degree and speak quite well and some HARD-OF-HEARING people who are totally without hearing and do not speak very well. What is important is their public behavior as Deaf people or as hard-of-hearing people.

Deaf people do not, at the center, view themselves as disabled or handicapped. Instead their view of themselves is one of wholeness and completeness. They view themselves as competent individuals with a linguistic and cultural history. This way of viewing themselves is learned from other Deaf people and is an example of the knowledge which Deaf people share. It is not an "adjustment" to a "handicap" as others see it. Deaf people may, at times, allow themselves to be categorized as "disabled" out of social, economic, or political necessity. However, this adoption of a seemingly contradictory view of themselves does not diminish their sense of themselves as a culturally and linguistically sophisticated people.

CULTURAL RICHNESS

Deaf people have found ways to define and express themselves through their rituals, tales, performances, and everyday social encounters. The richness of their sign language affords them the possibilities of insight, invention, and irony. Their "oral" and written literature, poetry, and dramatic performance reflect their different world view and history.

One example of an "oral" history that has been passed down over the years has been the story of the founding fathers of the first school for Deaf children in the United States, the American School in Hartford, Connecticut. The story tells of a journey by ship across the Atlantic by Laurent Clerc and Thomas Hopkins Gallaudet, the two founding fathers. As the story goes, enroute from France to the United States, Clerc taught Gallaudet his native FSL and Gallaudet taught Clerc English. FSL was then introduced in the new school and through the years became an independent sign language which we now call American Sign Language. The symbols and motifs of a crossing by water, of traveling a long journey from an old world to a new world, and of bringing the culture of Deaf people in France to the new world have turned an "oral" history into a classic "folktale." At the heart of the folktale is that their language, and by extension, their lives, have roots not in spoken language, but in signed language.

ASL LITERATURE

It is sometimes assumed that ASL has no literature because it is not written (although most languages of the world are also not written). Most of society did not believe that ASL was a language until the 1970's with the result being that its literature was largely ignored and denied for hundreds of years. This has had the effect of constraining the development of a strong body of ASL literary analysis and criticism and sometimes stifled creativity as well.

Despite this, however, there is a rich ASL literature including a strong tradition of "oral" history and folktales. The tradition in ASL literature has been passed down from generation to generation by "carriers" of the literature. These Deaf people have learned it from older Deaf people, either verbatim or giving it an added creative touch of their own. ASL literature is also constantly being created by Deaf poets, storytellers, historians, translators (into English), film and video producers, and dramatists. Plays and evenings of ASL poetry and storytelling, once seen mostly in clubs, are now becoming more and more widely viewed in public performances and festivals. A growing body of such performances is now available on film and videotape.

Many of the themes in ASL literature relate to the social condition in which Deaf people find themselves in America. Their experience of living within a world designed for hearing people and their experience of coping with the world's treatment and attitude towards Deaf people often finds its way into the literature. As Deaf people's consciousness of their language and culture increases, their literature openly celebrates their heritage and voices their anger and dreams. Like the suppressed literatures of other minority groups in America, there is still much to discover and understand about ASL literature. But fortunately, as a student, there will be a great deal of live and recorded performances available to you today.

DEAF PEOPLE IN SOCIETY

Through language, folktales, jokes and many other cultural forms, Deaf people weave stories about who they are, where they come from, what they believe in, and how they plan their lives. Sometimes these cultural forms illuminate another side of the lives of

Deaf people—they live in a world surrounded by people who hear. This relationship is uneasy at times and is related to issues of power, control, and domination. A common joke told by Deaf people helps to understand how these issues are addressed in their daily lives.

A deaf couple check into a motel. They retire early. In the middle of the night, the wife wakes her husband complaining of a headache and asks him to go to the car and get some aspirin from the glove compartment. Groggy with sleep, he struggles to get up, puts on his robe, and goes out of the room to his car. He finds the aspirin, and with the bottle in hand he turns toward the motel. But he cannot remember which room is his. After thinking a moment, he returns to the car, places his hand on the horn, holds it down, and waits. Very quickly the motel rooms light up, all but one. It's his wife's room, of course. He locks up his car and heads toward the room without a light.

This joke is about how a Deaf person uses hearing people—and sound—to his advantage. But beneath the surface it is about a turnaround of the power hearing people often exert over Deaf people because they do not hear. The tension of living among hearing people, as reflected in his joke, is a constant in the lives of Deaf people. (A discussion of this joke also appears in a chapter of Carol Padden & Tom Humphries' *Deaf in America: Voices from a Culture,* 1988).

While Deaf people know that they must live within a world shaped by others, they also have their own ideas about how to do this. Their culture has beliefs about how to integrate, or at least, co-exist with hearing people. Deaf people do not choose complete assimilation into a hearing society. Their culture offers them ways to live among hearing people and maintain a view of themselves that is not based on a loss or a deficiency which is often attributed to them by hearing society. It is through their language that Deaf people feel they can maintain both a sense of control of their lives in interactions with hearing people and also give them social and economic access to the society at large.

SOCIAL ORGANIZATION AND COMMUNITY LIFE

What is it like to live in a Deaf community? Each local community will have its own character. There are some common social structures that are central to Deaf community life. For example, at one time, Deaf clubs existed and thrived all over the United States. These social and sports clubs were the places where one maintained ties to the community away from schools. Often they had their own clubrooms. (See Bernard Bragg and Eugene Bergman's *Tales from a Clubroom* and the video *The LACD Story* for a sense of life in these clubs.) In recent years, forces such as the economic difficulty of maintaining these clubs, the development of communication technologies for Deaf people, and increased access by Deaf people to other social structures in the U.S., have led to a less prominent role of the club in the life of the community.

One of the most significant developments in Deaf communities in recent years has been the establishment of community service agencies for Deaf people all over the U.S. These agencies have sprung up where there are large numbers of Deaf people and have various kinds of community functions including advocacy, direct services, information services, and counseling. They may also function as cultural centers, sponsoring and organizing festivals, art shows, and youth events among other things. Today, many communities are anchored by these centers rather than clubs.

A great deal of the recreational and athletic life of the community is organized by two national organizations with local chapters, the World Recreation Association of the Deaf (WRAD) and the American Athletic Association of the Deaf (AAAD). Thousands of Deaf people belong to these organizations and others like them and they are extremely active and vital entities. Some of these organizations are open and welcoming to people who hear and can be a source for expanding your interaction with Deaf people as you learn ASL. However, some do have rules about participation such as the "deaf only" rule for engaging in AAAD competition.

There are other social and political organizations which have a large role in many Deaf communities. Among them are the local and state chapters of the National Association of the Deaf (NAD). These are social and political organizations of long standing which, by promoting, lobbying, educating the public, and defending Deaf people, have been responsible for many of the improvements in the quality of Deaf people's lives over the years.

As in any community, life in a Deaf community is one of choices. Deaf people individually choose the kind of social and cultural life they wish to fashion for themselves. It may be centered around the family, the church, sports, community activism, work, or any combination of choices available to communities. Whatever the choice, life in a Deaf community is vital and constant.

BEGINNING YOUR JOURNEY TO ASL

As you begin to study ASL, you will come into contact with the broad tapestry of Deaf people's culture and heritage. You will begin to better appreciate the complexities of the language and culture of Deaf people. A true appreciation of both comes only through association with Deaf people along with your classroom study. For those of you who want to read more or look for other resources, we have provided references at the end of this text as guidance.

LESSON 1

Personal Pronouns

1. The handshape for personal pronouns is the pointing index finger.
2. The locations for personal pronouns are:

I, me 	WE, us 
YOU 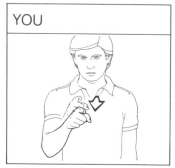	YOU-PL. 

The signer looks directly at the other person.

HE/SHE/IT, him, her 	THEY, them 

If the person or object is visible or nearby, the signer points in the direction of that person or object. If the person or object is not present, the signer can point to a location on either side.

Exercise 1.1:

Change the pronoun form from singular to plural, or from plural to singular.

EXAMPLES:

A. I
    WE
B. THEY
    HE/SHE/IT

1. YOU	4. THEY	7. HE
2. SHE	5. IT	8. I
3. WE	6. YOU-PL.	

Basic Sentence Structure: Sentences with Predicate Adjectives

1. It is common in simple sentences to repeat the subject pronoun at the end of the sentence.

EXAMPLES:

A. I HAPPY I. 'I am happy.'

B. SHE TIRED SHE. 'She is tired.'
C. HE SMART HE. 'He is smart.'

2. The following two forms are possible also:

EXAMPLES:

A.   I HAPPY.   'I am happy.'

B.   HAPPY I.   'I am happy.'

Exercise 1.2:

Following the example given, form new sentences from the pronouns and adjectives listed below.

EXAMPLE:

I, HAPPY
   I HAPPY I.   'I am happy.'
   I HAPPY.   'I am happy.'
   HAPPY I.   'I am happy.'

1. YOU, TALL
2. IT, HEAVY
3. I, SURPRISED
4. THEY, DEAF
5. YOU, HEARING
6. I, MAD
7. SHE, SLEEPY

8. WE, DEAF
9. IT, LIGHT
10. YOU, HAPPY
11. WE, SURPRISED
12. HE, INTERESTING
13. YOU, PRETTY
14. IT, UGLY

15. I, SHORT
16. THEY, SURPRISED
17. IT, BIG

18. I, SLEEPY
19. IT, SMALL
20. SHE, DEAF

Vocabulary

AND

ANGRY, furious

BEAUTIFUL

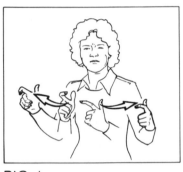

BIG, large

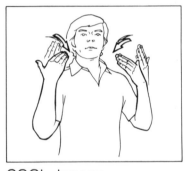

COOL, breeze

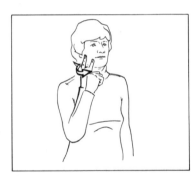

DEAF

DEAF

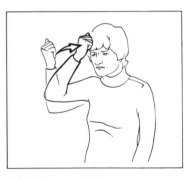

DUMB, stupid

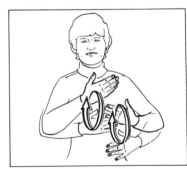

HAPPY

smart:
middle finger to
head, turn
out

hearing:
loop around mouth
w/ pointer

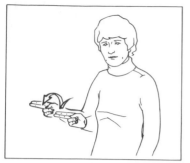

HARD-OF-HEARING

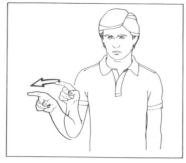

HE,SHE,IT, him, her

HEARING, SAY, speech

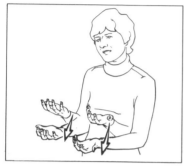

HEAVY

HELLO, hi

I, me

close middle finger to thumb

INTERESTING, interest

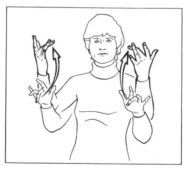

LIGHT (weight)

MAD, angry

PRETTY, beautiful

SAD

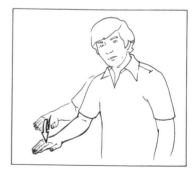

SHORT (height), small

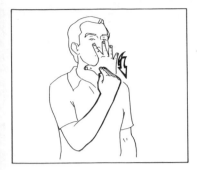

SLEEPY, drowsy

SMALL, little

SMART, clever, bright

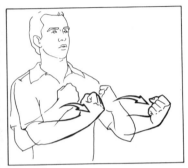

STRONG, strength, powerful

STUPID, ignorant, dumb

SURPRISED, amazed

TALL   *object*

TALL   *person*

THEY, them

TIRED, exhausted

UGLY

WARM

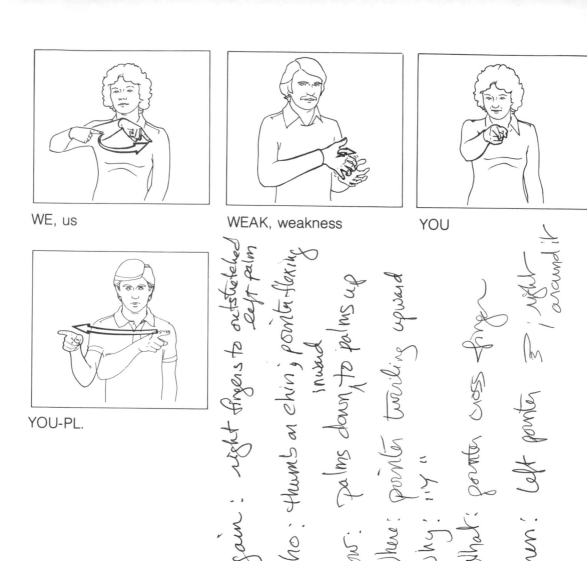

WE, us

WEAK, weakness

YOU

YOU-PL.

again: right fingers to outstretched left palm

who: thumb on chin; pointer flexing inward

How: palms down to palms up

Where: pointer twirling upward

why: "y"

What: pointer cross finger

when: left pointer ﹃; right 1 around it

YES — fist nods

NO — 2 fingers to thumb

What — pointer across palm

question — draw question mark w/ pointer

thank you / good — fingers to ~~mouth~~ chin → palm out

1. alphabet
2. 5 sentences (try out)

but: *cross* pointers together ^then apart ↔

went: point away w/ two hands

boring: pointer on nose ↻

work: fists in T-shap ("clap")

shool: palms horiz. together (clap)

pointer ~~waving~~ (*circling* ~~upward~~) = where

(past tense) finished =

−er = palms facing each other ↓ ↓

poor: elbow L pull on

love: *fingers of* pads of both hands to chest

saw: pointer + middle away eyes

LESSON 12

Possessives

The handshape for possessives is the 5-hand, fingers together. The locations are the same as personal pronouns. The palm moves in the direction of the "owner."

MY, mine 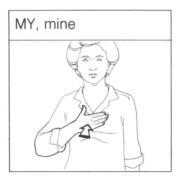	**OUR, ours** 
YOUR, yours 	**YOUR-PL., yours** 
HIS/HER/ITS, hers 	**THEIR, theirs** 

Exercise 2.1:

Change the personal pronouns listed below to possessives.

EXAMPLE:

I
   MY

1. YOU
2. SHE
3. WE
4. THEY
5. YOU-PL.

6. IT
7. ME
8. HE
9. HIM
10. THEM

Basic Sentence Structure: Sentences with Identifying Nouns

Simple sentences with nouns which identify the subject (predicate nominatives) are commonly structured like the simple sentences with predicate adjectives. The subject pronoun can be repeated at the end of the sentence.

EXAMPLES:

A. SHE TEACHER SHE.   'She is a teacher.'

B. SHE STUDENT.   'She is a student.'
C. MY MOTHER SHE.   'She is my mother.'

with: fists facing together: in circle

Exercise 2.2:

Following the example given, form new sentences from the following list.

EXAMPLES:

A. MY, MOTHER
   SHE MY MOTHER.   'She is my mother.'
B. WOMAN
   SHE WOMAN SHE.   'She is a woman.'

1. MY, SISTER
2. MY, BROTHER
3. YOUR, FATHER
4. OUR, FATHER
5. MY, GRANDMOTHER
6. MY, FRIEND
7. YOUR, GRANDFATHER
8. YOUR, TEACHER
9. MY, STUDENT
10. MY, FRIEND
11. BOY
12. GIRL
13. MAN
14. WOMAN

Using Two Third Person Pronouns

When pronouns are used in a sentence to refer to two different persons, point to a different location for each person. If the persons are not present, the signer can refer to one person on one side of the signer and the other person on the opposite side.

EXAMPLE:

HE HIS TEACHER HE.   'He is his teacher.'

Exercise 2.3:

Following the example given, form new sentences from the pronouns and nouns listed below.

EXAMPLE:

HER, BROTHER
   HE HER BROTHER HE.   'He is her brother.'

1. HER, SISTER
2. HER, MOTHER
3. SHE, THEIR, TEACHER
4. HIS, GRANDMOTHER
5. HER, FRIEND

6. HIS, STUDENT
7. HE, HER, BROTHER
8. HIS, FATHER
9. HER, GRANDFATHER
10. SHE, HIS, SISTER

NOTE: Use of AGENT Suffix

As with TEACHER and STUDENT, the AGENT suffix can be added to a sign to indicate profession or identity.

EXAMPLES: Profession

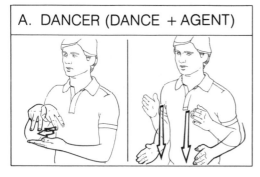

A. DANCER (DANCE + AGENT)

B. COOK (COOK + AGENT)

EXAMPLE: Identity

C. AMERICAN (AMERICA + AGENT)

log cabin

25

Vocabulary

AMERICA

AUNT

BOY, man

BROTHER or *boy to pointers ||*

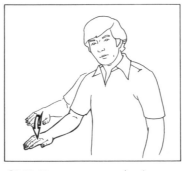

CHILD, short [*children sveral X*]

COOK, bake

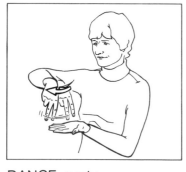

DANCE, party

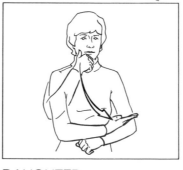

DAUGHTER

FAMILY

FATHER

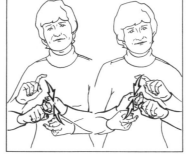

FRIEND

GIRL

 GOOD-FRIEND *(stay clasped)*

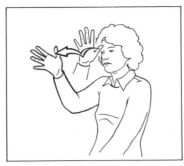 GRANDFATHER

 GRANDMOTHER

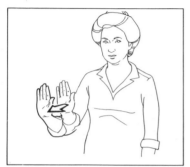 HIS, HERS, ITS

 HUSBAND

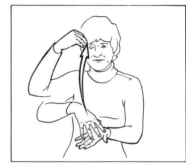 LEARN, acquire

 MAN

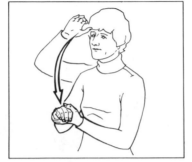 MOTHER

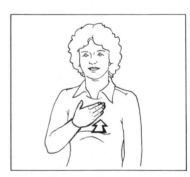 MY, mine

 NEPHEW "n"

 NIECE "n"

 OUR, ours

PARENTS

PLEASE

SISTER

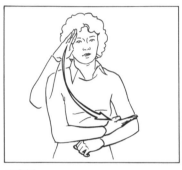

SON

STUDENT

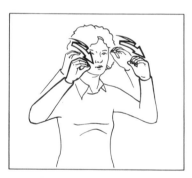

TEACH, educate

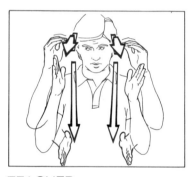

TEACHER

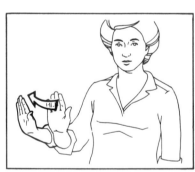

THEIR, theirs

UNCLE

WIFE

WOMAN

28

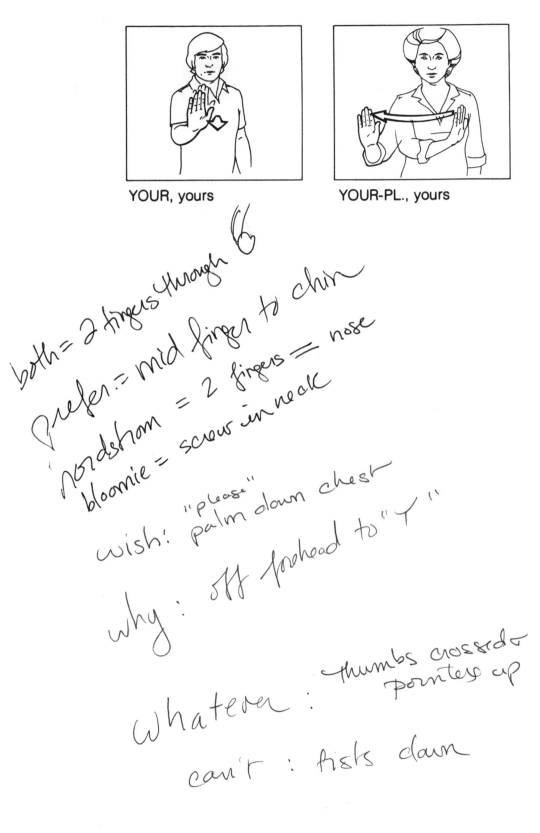

YOUR, yours   YOUR-PL., yours

both = 2 fingers through

prefer = mid finger to chin

nordstrom = 2 fingers = nose

bloomie = screw in neck

wish: "please"
palm down chest

why: off forehead to "Y"

whatever: thumbs crossed
pointers up

can't: fists down

LESSON 3

Basic Sentence Structure: Sentences with Verbs

A common sentence structure with verbs is Subject + Verb + Object.

EXAMPLES:

A. I HAVE BOOK I.   'I have a book.'

B. HE NEED MONEY HE.   'He needs money.'
C. SHE WANT CAR SHE.   'She wants a car.'

Exercise 3.1:

Using the example given, substitute verbs from the list below.

EXAMPLE:

I HAVE BOOK I.   'I have a book.'
NEED
   I NEED BOOK I.   'I need a book.'

1. FORGET
2. REMEMBER
3. LIKE
4. KNOW

5. WANT
6. HAVE
7. READ
8. LOSE

9. FIND
10. ENJOY

Basic Sentence Structure: Pronouns and Nouns

Pronouns are often used together with nouns. In these cases, the pronoun can function like the English word, <u>the</u>, to specify. The pronoun can occur either before or after the noun.

EXAMPLES:

A. MAN HE KNOW ME HE. 'The man knows me.'

B. SHE WOMAN HAVE MY BOOK SHE. 'The woman has my book.'

EXERCISE 3.2:

Using the example given, substitute signs from the list below.

EXAMPLE:

MAN HE KNOW ME HE. 'The man knows me.'
  WOMAN
    <u>WOMAN</u> SHE KNOW ME SHE. 'The woman knows me.'
  LIKE
    WOMAN SHE <u>LIKE</u> ME SHE. 'The woman likes me.'
  BOOK
    WOMAN SHE LIKE <u>BOOK</u> SHE. 'The woman likes the book.'

1. REMEMBER	11. MAN
2. YOUR NAME	12. PRACTICE
3. FORGET	13. WOMAN
4. BOOK	14. HAVE, CHAIR
5. BOY	15. NEED
6. HAVE	16. CAR
7. PAPER	17. MAN, MONEY
8. NEED	18. WANT
9. GIRL	19. GIRL, BOOK
10. REMEMBER, SIGN	20. HAVE

Basic Sentence Structure: Adjectives and Nouns

Adjectives appear either before or after the noun.

EXAMPLES:

A. I WANT BOX RED I. 'I want a red box.'

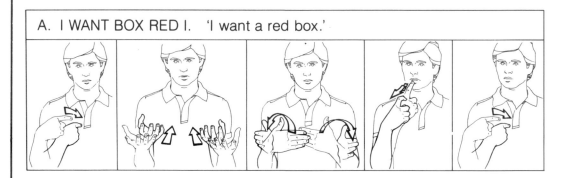

I WANT RED BOX I. 'I want a red box.'

B. I REMEMBER CAR BLUE I.   'I remember a blue car.'
   I REMEMBER BLUE CAR I.   'I remember a blue car.'

Exercise 3.3:

To the following sentences add the adjective following the noun.

EXAMPLE:

I HAVE CAR I.   'I have a car.'
  (BLUE)
    I HAVE CAR BLUE I.   'I have a blue car.'

1. I READ BOOK.   (INTERESTING)

2. HE HAVE HOME HE.   (PRETTY)

3. SHE WANT CHAIR.   (BLUE)

4. I REMEMBER MAN.   (TALL)

5. HE LOSE BOOK HE.   (GREEN)

6. THEY FIND BOX.   (SMALL)

7. HE WANT TABLE.   (NEW)

8. I NEED PAPER FOR CLASS I.   (YELLOW)

9. I KNOW WOMAN I.   (DEAF)

10. SHE LIKE CAR SHE.   (SMALL)

Exercise 3.4:

Repeat Exercise 3.3 with the adjective before the noun.

EXAMPLE:

I HAVE CAR I.   'I have a car.'
  (BLUE)
    I HAVE BLUE CAR I.   'I have a blue car.'

Descriptive Adjectives

There are some signs called <u>classifiers</u> which are used to represent the size and shape of an object. Variations in the form of classifiers can be used to show the relative size of objects.

CL:F

For small, flat and round objects such as a coin, a button, a watch.

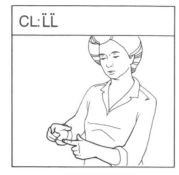

CL:L̈L̈

For flat and round objects such as a pancake, a small dish or plate, a hamburger.

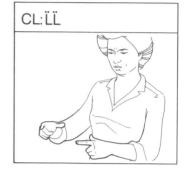

CL:L̈L̈

For larger flat and round objects such as a large plate, a big steak, a large puddle.

CL:C

For small container-like objects such as a cup, a glass, a bottle, a vase, a can.

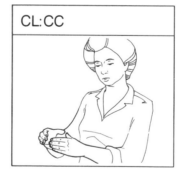

CL:CC

For container-like objects such as a bowl, a large can, a thick cable.

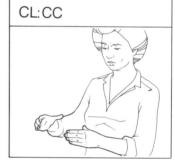

CL:CC

For larger container-like objects such as a pail, a large bowl, a hat box.

CL:BB

For objects with a flat surface such as the top of a small table, or a shelf.

CL:BB

For longer objects with a flat surface such as a long board, a long shelf, a long table, a plot of land.

When using sentences with descriptive classifiers, the signer looks at the classifier.

EXAMPLE:

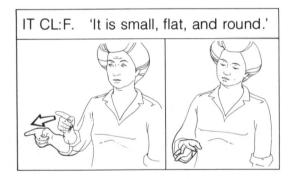

IT CL:F.   'It is small, flat, and round.'

Exercise 3.5:

For the objects listed below, give the appropriate classifier.

EXAMPLE:

'coin'
   IT CL:F.   'It is small, flat, and round.'

1. 'long sheet of paper'
2. 'tortilla'

3. 'round mint'
4. 'unfolded map'

5. 'fabric on floor'
6. 'platter'
7. 'beer can'
8. 'manhole cover'

9. 'bucket'
10. 'soap dish'
11. 'cereal bowl'
12. 'Susan B. Anthony dollar'

Vocabulary

Classifiers: can act out instead of
spelling out he went to her, point to
"he" use pointer and move to "her"
# of people = # fingers ∴ show it!
cars can do same → act out w/ hands

ABOUT, concerning

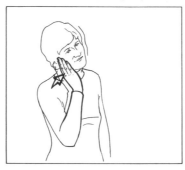

BED

BLACK, Black-person

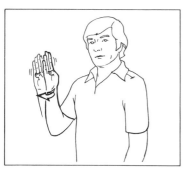

BLUE

BOOK

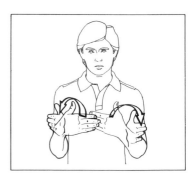

BOX, package, room

BROWN

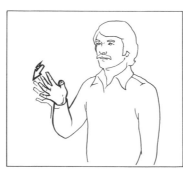

BROWN

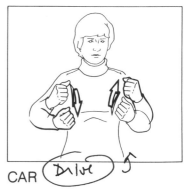

CAR (Drive) ʃ

↳ 3 fingers on
side

CHAIR, seat

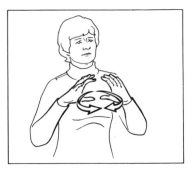

CLASS, GROUP, team

COLOR

DIALOGUE, talk with

ENJOY, appreciate

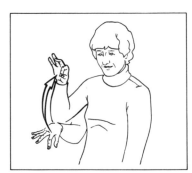

FIND, discover

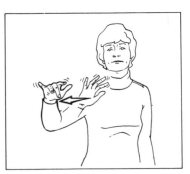

FINGERSPELL

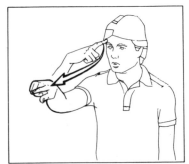

FOR

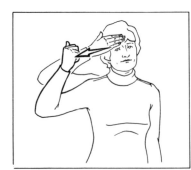

FORGET

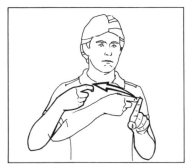

FROM

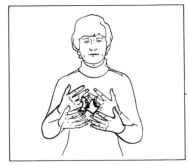

GRAY

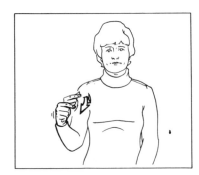

GREEN

HAVE, own, possess

HOME

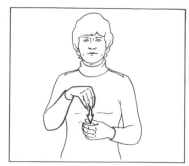

IN, contained in

KNOW, aware, conscious

LIKE

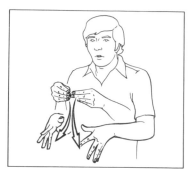

LOSE

MONEY, financial, economic

NAME

NEED, necessary

(tapping on shoulder)

NEW, modern

OLD, age

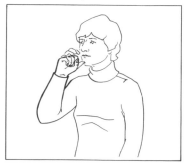

ORANGE

38

PAPER, page

PRACTICE, exercise, train, rehearse

READ

RED

REMEMBER

SIGN, sign language

TABLE, desk

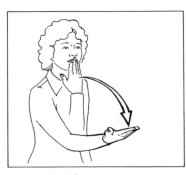

THANK-YOU

WANT, desire

WHITE

WHITE-PERSON

YELLOW

LESSON 4

Negatives

There are several ways to form negative sentences. All are accompanied by a negative marker, _____ n _____ , which is:
1. a headshake
2. eyebrows squeezed together

The different forms of negative sentences are:

  1. Use of NOT.   NOT either comes before the verb or at the end of the sentence.

    EXAMPLES:

                _____ n _____
    A. I REMEMBER GIRL NOT I. 'I don't remember the girl.'

                _____ n _____
    B. I NOT REMEMBER GIRL I. 'I don't remember the girl.'
                _____ n _____
    C. HE NEED MONEY NOT HE. 'He doesn't need money.'
                _____ n _____
    D. HE NOT NEED MONEY HE. 'He doesn't need money.'

  2. Use of Negative Incorporation. The negative of these verbs, KNOW, WANT, and LIKE, are formed by incorporating an outward, twisting movement.

EXAMPLES:

   _____ n _____
A. I DON'T-KNOW WOMAN I.   'I don't know the woman.'

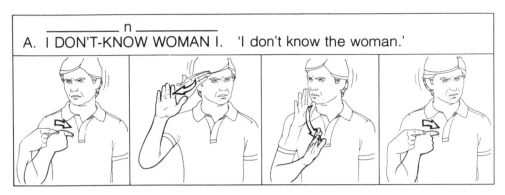

   _____ n _____
B. DON'T-WANT MONEY SHE.   'She doesn't want the money.'
   _____ n _____
C. HE DON'T-LIKE BOOK HE.   'He doesn't like the book.'

3. Use of Negative Marker. _____ n _____ may be used alone to negate a simple sentence.

EXAMPLES:

   __ n _____
A. I READ BOOK I.   'I'm not reading the book.'

   _____ n _____
B. I UNDERSTAND MOVIE I.   'I don't understand the movie.'

Exercise 4.1:

Change the following sentences to negative sentences by adding NOT or a negative incorporation in addition to the negative marker.

EXAMPLES:

A. I KNOW WOMAN I.   'I know the woman.'
   _____ n _____
   I DON'T-KNOW WOMAN I.   'I don't know the woman.'

B. SHE FEEL GOOD SHE.   'She feels well.'
   _____ n _____
   SHE FEEL GOOD NOT SHE.   'She doesn't feel well.'
   _____ n _____
   SHE NOT FEEL GOOD SHE.   'She doesn't feel well.'

1. HE LIKE MOVIE HE.

2. DAUGHTER SHE LIKE SCHOOL SHE.

3. I SEE DOG I.

4. IT SMELL GOOD IT.

5. I UNDERSTAND BOOK I.

6. THEY BELIEVE YOU.

7. CAT IT HUNGRY IT.

8. HOUSE IT EXPENSIVE IT.

9. IT FOOD HOT IT.

10. WOMAN SHE WANT T-T-Y SHE.

11. SHE KNOW SIGN SHE.

12. BOY HE LOSE MONEY HE.

13. CAR IT BLUE IT.

Exercise 4.2:

Change the following sentences to negative sentences by using only the negative marker.

EXAMPLE:

I REMEMBER YOUR HOUSE I.   'I remember your house.'
   _____ n _____
   I REMEMBER YOUR HOUSE I.   'I don't remember your house.'

1. I TIRED I.

2. YOU UNDERSTAND ME.

3. GIRL HAVE BOOK SHE.

4. MY SISTER FIND MONEY.

5. I SMELL IT I.

6. I WORK I.

7. THEY PRACTICE SIGN.

Yes/No Questions

Questions that ask for a "Yes" or "No" answer are made by simultaneously:
1. Raising the eyebrows.
2. Moving the head slightly forward.
3. Looking directly at the person being asked the question.
   _____q _____ will be used to represent the above grammatical features of Yes/No questions.

EXAMPLE:

Statement: SURPRISED ME.   YOU REMEMBER MY NAME YOU. 'I'm surprised. You remember my name.'

_____q_____
Question: YOU REMEMBER MY NAME YOU? 'Do you remember my name?'

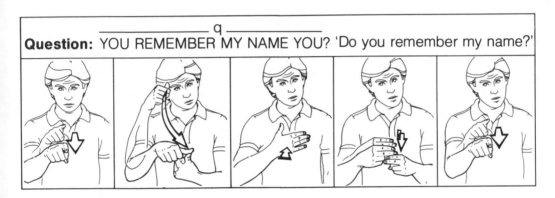

Exercise 4.3:

Change the following statements to questions.

EXAMPLE:

Statement: GRANDFATHER HAVE CHAIR.   'Grandfather has a chair.'

_____q_____
Question: GRANDFATHER HAVE CHAIR?   'Does Grandfather have a chair?'

1. HE LIKE WORK HE.

2. TEACHER LOSE MY PAPER.

3. IT HOUSE COLD IT.

4. GRANDMOTHER FIND MONEY.

5. IT CAT HUNGRY IT.

6. IT BOOK RIGHT IT.

7. DOG IT UNDERSTAND SIGN IT.

8. SHE KNOW MY NAME SHE.

9. BOY HE SHORT HE.

10. HE HEARING HE.

43

Responses to Yes/No Questions

When responding to Yes/No questions, a positive nod of the head accompanies the positive response (represented by _____ y _____), and the negative marker accompanies the negative response, The YES or NO signs may be dropped from the response. The following examples are appropriate responses to Yes/No questions.

EXAMPLES:

————————— q —————————
A. HE REMEMBER MY NAME HE?   'Does he remember my name?'

——————— y ———————
YES, HE REMEMBER HE.   'Yes, he does.'

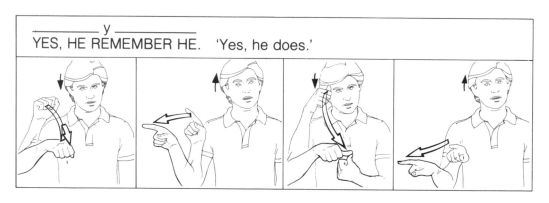

——————— n ———————
NO, HE NOT REMEMBER HE.   'No, he doesn't.'

_____q_____
B. SHE NEED MONEY? 'Does she need money?'

_____y_____
YES, SHE NEED. 'Yes, she does.'

_____n_____
NO, SHE NOT NEED. 'No, she doesn't.'

_____q_____
C. SHE KNOW SIGN SHE? 'Does she know how to sign?'

_____y_____
SHE KNOW SHE. 'Yes, she does.'

_____n_____
SHE DON'T-KNOW SHE. 'No, she doesn't.'

_____q_____
D. YOU SLEEPY? 'Are you sleepy?'

_____y_____
YES, I SLEEPY I. 'Yes, I am.'

_____n_____
NO, I NOT SLEEPY I. 'No, I'm not.'

There is an additional appropriate negative response to Yes/No questions with predicate adjectives such as

_____q_____
YOU DEAF YOU?

_____n_____
NO, I NOT I. 'No, I'm not.'

Exercise 4.4:

Form appropriate responses to the following questions.

EXAMPLE:

_____q_____
Question: GRANDFATHER HAVE CHAIR HE? 'Does Grandfather have a chair?'
_____y_____
Response: YES, HE HAVE HE. 'Yes, he does.'

45

Question	Response
_____ q _____ 1. HE LIKE WORK HE?	NO,...
_____ q _____ 2. TEACHER LOSE MY PAPER?	NO,...
_____ q _____ 3. IT HOUSE COLD IT?	YES,...
_____ q _____ 4. GRANDMOTHER FIND MONEY?	YES,...
_____ q _____ 5. IT CAT SICK IT?	NO,...
_____ q _____ 6. IT BOOK RIGHT IT?	NO,...
_____ q _____ 7. DOG IT UNDERSTAND SIGN IT?	YES,...
_____ q _____ 8. SHE KNOW MY NAME SHE?	YES,...
_____ q _____ 9. HE HEARING HE?	YES,...
_____ q _____ 10. BOY HE SHORT HE?	NO,...

Negative Questions

Yes/No questions which contain negatives are made like other Yes/No questions except that the raised eyebrows are squeezed together and a negative headshake is used throughout the question. _____ nq _____ will be used to represent the above-mentioned grammatical features of negative questions.

EXAMPLES:

_____ nq _____
A. HE HAPPY NOT HE?   'He's not happy?'

_____ nq _____
B. YOU EAT YOU?   'You aren't eating?'

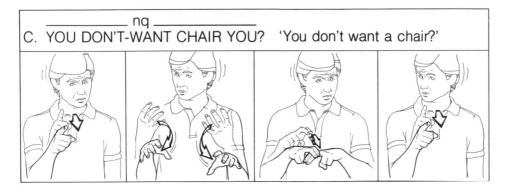

_____ nq _____
C. YOU DON'T-WANT CHAIR YOU?   'You don't want a chair?'

Exercise 4.5:

Change the following negative statements to negative questions.

EXAMPLE:

_____ n _____
Statement: HE TIRED NOT HE.   'He's not tired.'

_____ nq _____
Question: HE TIRED NOT HE?   'He's not tired?'

_____ n _____
1. YOU UNDERSTAND ME.

_____ n _____
2. SHE SEE MOVIE NOT.

_____ n _____
3. HE DEAF HE.

_____ n _____
4. SHE DON'T-WANT CAT.

_____ n _____
5. HE DON'T-KNOW MY SISTER HE.

_____ n _____
6. IT DIRTY NOT IT.

_____ n _____
7. HE NOT AMERICAN HE.

47

Vocabulary

AWFUL, terrible

BAD, unfortunate

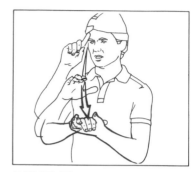
BELIEVE

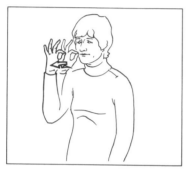
CAT

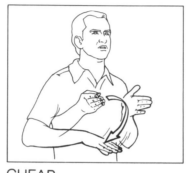
CHEAP

CLEAN, (NICE) pure
↳strike hand

COLD, (WINTER — two "ko's" facing)

DIRTY

DOG (or) pat leg

DON'T-KNOW

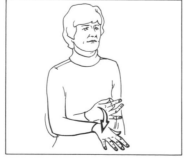
DON'T-LIKE

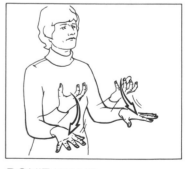
DON'T-WANT

48

EAT, FOOD

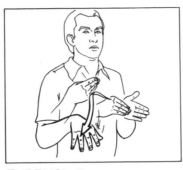

EXPENSIVE

EXPLAIN, describe

FEEL, feelings, (sense) *touch chest* *rub finger*

GOOD

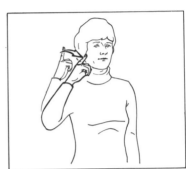

HEAR, sound

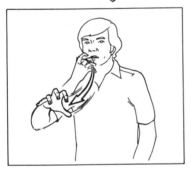

HOT, heat

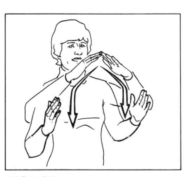

HOUSE

HUH?

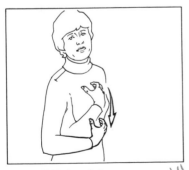

HUNGRY, wish

LANGUAGE

LESSON, COURSE, chapter

bump hit palm 2x

NYC = rub "y" across palm

49

Then = L on side, pointer touch thumb point

LOVE

MEET

MOVIE

NO

NOT

OH-I-SEE, oh *(nod it)*

RIGHT, correct

SCHOOL

SEE, sight

high school = h+s
college - off hand up
univ w/u

sight seeing
see + Us
(nature)

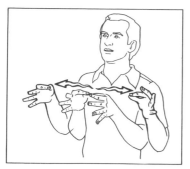
SENTENCE, language

SICK

SMELL, odor

SORRY, regret

TASTE, prefer, favorite

delicious = snap w/ mid & thumb

UNDERSTAND, comprehend

WELL, so

so what?

WORD, (vocabulary)

letter = bounce L → bounce √ off pointer

WORK, JOB

WORLD

WRONG   *(tap)*

YES

YOUNG, youth   *stroke chest*

alone/always/some thing = finger (pointer in loop)   twist wrist

nothing = 2 zeros

where = wiggle pointer

to do = "clap" pointer w/ thumb

51

NOTES

lion
skunk
horse
cow / bull
mouse
cat
dog
kangaroo (Australia)
rabbit
deer
tiger
snake
elephant
giraffe
mouse / Mickey
pig
monkey / gorilla

dolphin
whale
fish
shark

bird
spider
bug

(lizard?)

slow down   shiding rt on ~~back~~ of left (slow)
point rt down (down)

DIALOGUE 1

Tom is introducing Betty to Jack. In a typical first meeting between Deaf people, there are requests of information about each other's background. This includes information about where one is from, family connections, where one went to school, and who one knows in the deaf community. This information helps to place and center the individuals in the culture and community.

Jack: HELLO.   SHE FRIEND YOUR SHE?
                                                _____q_____

Tom: YES.   SHE NAME B-E-T-T-Y S-M-I-T-H.   SHE FROM I-N-D.
        _ y _

Jack: I HAPPY I-MEET-YOU.   MY NAME J-A-C-K J-O-N-E-S.   I FROM M-I-N-N.

Betty: HAPPY I-MEET-YOU.   YOU HAVE BROTHER NAME B-O-B J-O-N-E-S?
                                                       _____q_____

Jack: YES.   YOU KNOW HE YOU?
       _ y _   _____q_____

Betty: I KNOW HE I.
        _____y____

Tom: WELL DEAF SMALL WORLD.

53

LESSON 5

Basic Sentence Structure: Present and Past Tense

1. The form for present tense is:

I WORK I.   'I am working.'

Also, a tense indicator such as NOW or TODAY may be used either at the beginning of the sentence or at the end of the sentence:

EXAMPLES:

A. NOW I WORK I.   'I am working now.'

I WORK NOW I.   'I am working now.'

B. TODAY I VISIT GRANDMOTHER.   'I am visiting Grandmother today.'
    I VISIT GRANDMOTHER TODAY.   'I am visiting Grandmother today.'

2. A tense indicator may also be used to establish past tense:

EXAMPLES:

A. YESTERDAY I WORK I. 'I worked yesterday.'

B. BEFORE I GO I. 'I went before.'

Some other past tense markers are:

1. RECENTLY   'in the recent past'
2. BEFORE   'in the past, used to'
3. LONG-AGO   'in the distant past'
4. YESTERDAY   'yesterday'

Exercise 5.1:

Change the following sentences to past tense using the tense indicator given at the beginning of the sentence.

EXAMPLE:

I WORK I. 'I am working.'
(YESTERDAY)
   YESTERDAY I WORK I. 'I worked yesterday.'

1. I PRACTICE SIGN I.   (YESTERDAY)

2. HE BUY CAR HE.   (RECENTLY)

3. BOY HE STUDENT HE.   (BEFORE)

4. SHE DIE SHE, SORRY.   (YESTERDAY)

55

5. I TEACH RESIDENTIAL SCHOOL I.   (LONG-AGO)

6. WOMAN SHE LOSE P-I-N CL:F.   (RECENTLY)

7. $\overline{\text{I NOT READ YOUR}}^{n} \overline{\text{HOMEWORK.}}$ (YESTERDAY)

8. HE LEARN SIGN HE.   (RECENTLY)

9. SHE HEARING SCHOOL.   (BEFORE)

10. SHE VISIT WASHINGTON SHE.   (LONG-AGO)

Basic Sentence Structure: Using FINISH

It is also possible to use FINISH to show that an action has been completed. FINISH appears either before or after the verb.

EXAMPLES:

A. I FINISH SEE MOVIE.   'I have seen the movie.' or 'I already saw the movie.'

B. I SEE FINISH MOVIE.   'I have seen the movie.' or 'I already saw the movie.'

Exercise 5.2:

Change the following sentences to the past with FINISH.

EXAMPLE:

I BUY CAR. 'I am buying a car.'
  I BUY CAR FINISH. 'I bought a car.'

1. HE FATHER MAKE COOKIE HE.

2. SHE WRITE PAPER SHE.

3. BROTHER READ BOOK HE.

4. I SELL HOUSE I.

5. MOVIE I SEE I.

6. I VISIT GRANDMOTHER I.

7. MY SIGN IMPROVE.

8. HE DRINK WATER HE.

9. SON HE GROW-UP HE.

10. I COOK ALL-DAY I.

Basic Sentence Structure: Future Tense

Some future tense indicators are:

1. AFTER-AWHILE 'in the near future'
2. WILL 'in the future'
3. LATER 'in the future'
4. FUTURE 'in the far future'
5. TOMORROW 'tomorrow'

EXAMPLES:

A. TOMORROW I GO-AWAY I. 'I will go tomorrow.'

I GO-AWAY TOMORROW. 'I will go tomorrow.'

57

B. I EAT WILL I. 'I will eat.'

Exercise 5.3:

Change the following past tense sentences to future tense using the future tense indicators given.

EXAMPLE:

YESTERDAY I BUY CAR I. 'Yesterday I bought a car.'
  (WILL)
    I BUY CAR WILL I. 'I will buy a car.'

1. YESTERDAY I PRACTICE SIGN I. (TOMORROW)

2. LONG-AGO I GO COLLEGE I. (WILL)

3. RECENTLY I TO-TELEPHONE YOU I. (LATER)

4. RECENTLY HE LEARN SIGN HE. (WILL)

5. BEFORE COOKIE CL:ÏL I MAKE I. (FUTURE)

6. T-T-Y SHE BUY SHE. (AFTER-AWHILE)

7. I SEE MOVIE FINISH I. (TOMORROW)

8. YESTERDAY PANTS I WEAR I. (WILL)

9. BEFORE MOTHER STAY 1-WEEK. (WILL)

NOTE: Establishing the Tense Context

Once the context of tense is established through the use of a tense indicator, it is not necessary to repeat the tense indicator in later sentences until a change in tense is desired.

EXAMPLES:

A. NOW I WORK I.   'I am working.'
   I TEACHER I.   'I am a teacher.'
   I LIKE TEACH I.   'I like teaching.'

B. YESTERDAY I SICK I.   'I was sick yesterday.'
   I STAY HOME I.   'I stayed home.'
   MOTHER SHE TO-TELEPHONE DOCTOR SHE.   'My mother telephoned the doctor.'

C. TOMORROW I SELL MY CAR I.   'Tomorrow I will sell my car.'
   _____ n _____
   I NOT BUY NEW CAR I.   'I'm not going to buy a new car.'
   I WALK WORK I.   'I will walk to work.'

Vocabulary

AFTER-AWHILE, later

AFTERNOON

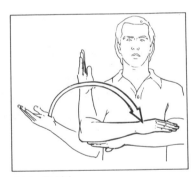
ALL-DAY

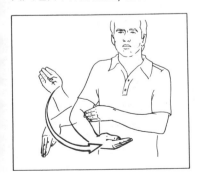
ALL-NIGHT, overnight

BEFORE, previous

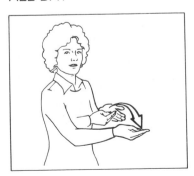
BUY

59

COLLEGE, university

COOKIE

DAY

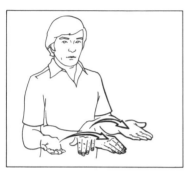

DIE, dead, death

DOCTOR w/d
nurse w/n

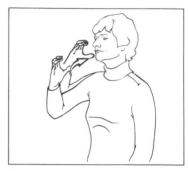

DRINK

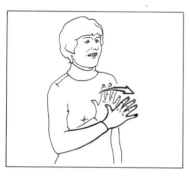

FINE

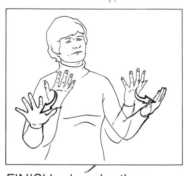

FINISH, already, then

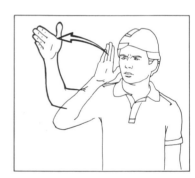

FUTURE

GO-AWAY, leave

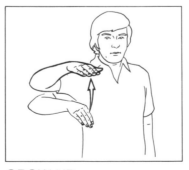

GROW-UP

HOMEWORK

60

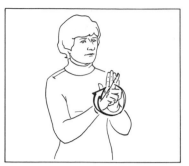

1-HOUR, hour

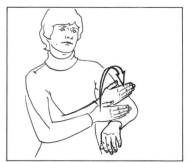

IMPROVE

opposite = downward

LATER

LETTER, mail

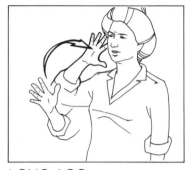

LONG-AGO

no good = "ng" flick

send = go away w/ palm down

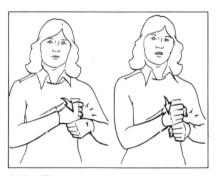

MAKE

1-MINUTE, minute

1-MONTH, month

MORNING

NIGHT, TONIGHT

OR : point back + forth
Then : sideways ; point thumb, pointer

NOON

NOW

NOW

PANTS

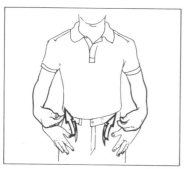

RECENTLY, just awhile ago

RESIDENTIAL-SCHOOL, institute

SELL *also "shop"*

STAY

TODAY

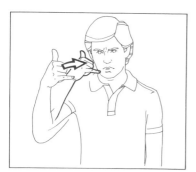

TO-TELEPHONE, call

TOMORROW

USED-TO, formerly

62

don't care = pointer to nose

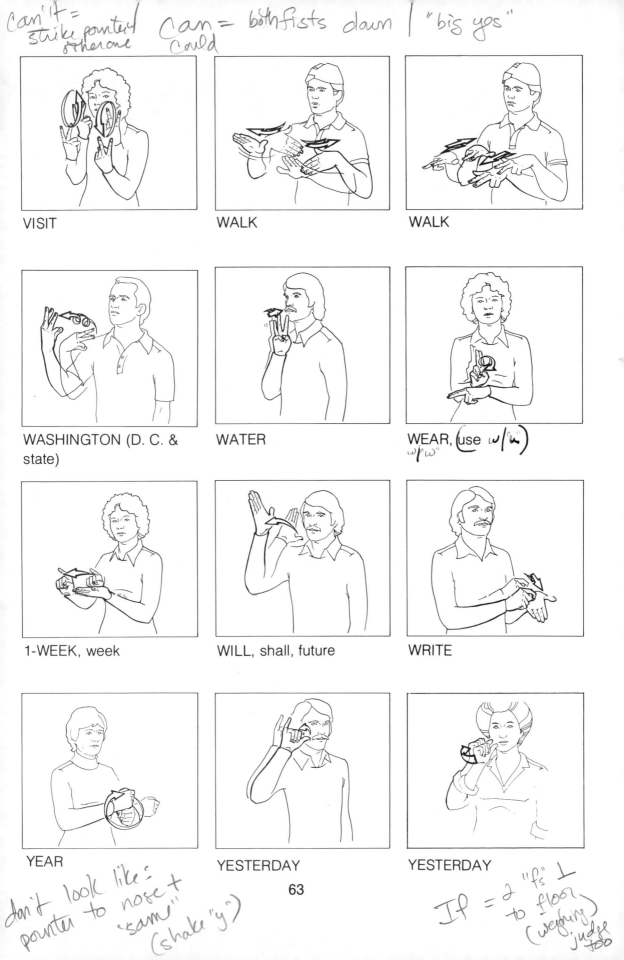

VISIT

WALK

WALK

WASHINGTON (D. C. & state)

WATER

WEAR, (use w/w)
w/w

1-WEEK, week

WILL, shall, future

WRITE

YEAR

YESTERDAY

YESTERDAY

LESSON 6

Basic Sentence Structure:
Object + Subject + Verb

1. Another common sentence structure is: Object + Subject + Verb.

EXAMPLE:

_ t ___
IT BOOK GIRL HAVE.   'The girl has a book.'

In this sentence structure the object is signed first, and there is usually a topic marker while signing the object of the sentence. The topic marker, represented by _____ t _____, is raised eyebrows.

2. When using adjectives, the following forms are possible:

EXAMPLES:

_____ t _____
COFFEE BLACK SHE LIKE.   'She likes black coffee.'
_____ t _____
BLACK COFFEE SHE LIKE.   'She likes black coffee.'

Exercise 6.1:

Using the example given substitute signs from the list below.

EXAMPLE:

```
 __t__
COFFEE I LIKE I.   'I like coffee.'
   TEA
 _t_
TEA I LIKE I.   'I like tea.'
```

1. PREFER

2. HATE

3. WORK

4. ENJOY

5. T-V

6. LOOK-AT

7. BICYCLE

8. DON'T-LIKE

9. MEAT

10. NOT EAT

11. SWEET CL:ÏÏ

12. BUY

[handwritten note:] laws = palm up tap twice 2nd art

[handwritten note:] up toyou = pointer across br. to thumb (fist) down hard

Basic Sentence Structure: Directional and Non-Directional Verbs

Some verbs change their movement to indicate the subject and object of the verb—they incorporate the locations of the subject and object pronouns. These verbs are called directional verbs. Some of these verbs are:

SHOW	ASK	TELL	LOOK-AT
HELP	SEND	GIVE	PAY

EXAMPLES:

A. I I-GIVE-YOU MONEY.   'I am giving you money.'

B. YOU-GIVE-ME MONEY.   'You are giving me money.'

C. I I-ASK-YOU.   'I am asking you.'
D. YOU-ASK-ME.   'You are asking me.'

Note that object pronouns are not signed in these types of sentences except in emphatic forms.

E. YESTERDAY YOU-ASK-ME I NOT HE.   'You asked me yesterday, not him.'

There are other verbs such as KNOW, HAVE, WANT, NEED, and REMEMBER which do not change their movement to indicate the subject and object, and do not incorporate the location of the subject and object pronouns.

F. I KNOW YOU I.   'I know you.'
G. YOU KNOW I YOU.   'You know me.'
H. I REMEMBER YOU I.   'I remember you.'
I. YOU REMEMBER I YOU.   'You remember me.'

Exercise 6.2:

Change the following I to you verb forms to you to me verb forms.

EXAMPLE:

_ t __
BOOK YESTERDAY I I-GIVE-YOU.   'Yesterday I gave you the book.'
 _ t __
  BOOK YESTERDAY YOU-GIVE-ME.   'Yesterday you gave me the book.'

 _ t __
1. TICKET TOMORROW I I-PAY-YOU.

66

```
        _ t _
2. LETTER LATER I I-SEND-YOU.

        _____ t _____
3. RIGHT ADDRESS TOMORROW I I-TELL-YOU.

        _____ t _____
4. TELETYPEWRITER NEW I I-SHOW-YOU WILL I.

5. I FINISH I-ASK-YOU.

        _ t _
6. LETTER I I-HELP-YOU WRITE WILL I.

7. I I-GIVE-YOU PICTURE NOW.

8. AFTER-AWHILE I AGAIN I-ASK-YOU.

        _____ t _____
9. PRETTY CL:L̈L̈ I I-SHOW-YOU WILL I.

        ____ t ____
10. UMBRELLA LONG-AGO I I-GIVE-YOU.
```

Basic Sentence Structure: Directional Verbs Incorporating HE/SHE/IT

Directional verbs also incorporate the HE/SHE/IT pronoun locations.

EXAMPLES:

A. TOMORROW I I-GIVE-HER BOOK.   'Tomorrow I will give her the book.'

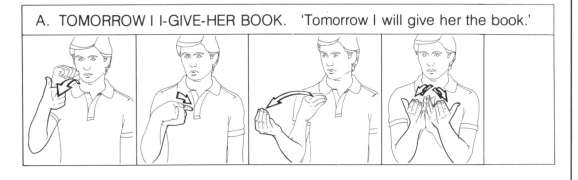

B. SHE-GIVE-ME   'she gives me'

C. YOU-GIVE-HER   'you give her'

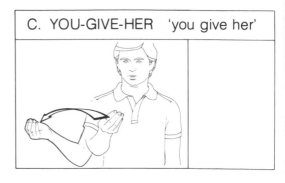

D. SHE-GIVE-YOU   'she gives you'

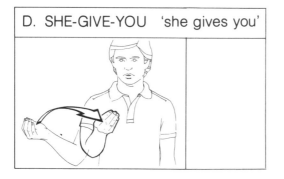

E. SHE-GIVE-HIM   'she gives him'

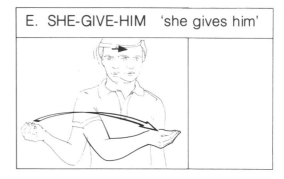

F. HE-GIVE-HER   'he gives her'

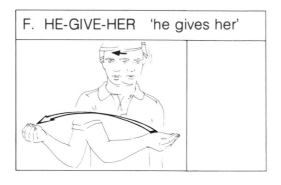

Exercise 6.3:

Change the following <u>I to her/him/it</u> verb forms to <u>she/he/it to me</u> verb forms.

EXAMPLE:

    ____ t ____
UMBRELLA TOMORROW I I-GIVE-HER.   'Tomorrow I'll give her an umbrella.'
     ____ t ____
  UMBRELLA TOMORROW SHE-GIVE-ME.   'Tomorrow she'll give me an um-
                                                      brella.'

1. YESTERDAY I I-TELL-HER STAY.

    ___ t ___
2. CLOTHES TOMORROW I I-HELP-HIM BUY.

3. FINISH I I-ASK-HIM WAIT.

    ___ t __
4. MOVIE LATER I I-SHOW-HER.

    ___ t ___
5. MONEY TOMORROW IT-SEND-HER.

Change the following you to <u>her/him/it</u> verb forms to <u>she/he/it</u> to you verb forms.

EXAMPLE:

    ___ t ___
UMBRELLA TOMORROW YOU-GIVE-HER. 'Tomorrow you'll give her an umbrella.'

    ___ t ___
UMBRELLA TOMORROW SHE-GIVE-YOU. 'Tomorrow she'll give you an umbrella.'

    _____ q _____
6. WILL YOU-ASK-HIM WORK?

    _____ q _____
7. BREAD TODAY YOU-HELP-HIM MAKE?

    _____ t _____
8. NEW WRISTWATCH YOU-SHOW-HIM NOW.

    _ t _
9. BOX YOU-SEND-HER LATER.

Directional Verbs with Classifiers

Some classifiers can add directional movement and become directional verbs. Two examples of these are:

CL:C	CL:C↑

For small container-like objects such as a cup, a glass, a bottle, or a vase.	For objects which can be held in the hand such as a book, a portable teletypewriter; a stack of papers, a small box.

EXAMPLES:

—— t ——
A. GLASS GIVE-CL:C-YOU.   'I'll give you a glass.'

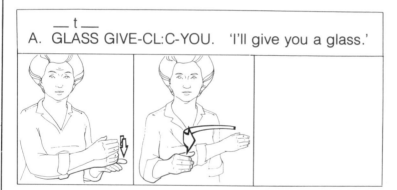

—— t ——
B. BOTTLE HE-GIVE-CL:C-ME WILL HE.   'He'll give me the bottle.'

_____ t _____
C. TOMORROW TELETYPEWRITER GIVE-CL:C↑-HIM.   'Tomorrow I'll give him
the portable teletypewriter.'

_____ t _____
D. A-B-C-A-S-L BOOK SHE-GIVE-CL:C↑-ME.   'She gave me the ABCASL
book.'

Exercise 6.4:

Use the appropriate C-classifier for the nouns given following the example below.
   EXAMPLE:
   MILK
      _ t _
      MILK GIVE-CL:C-YOU.   'I'll give you a glass of milk.'

1. BOX

2. PAPER

3. WATER

4. BOOK

5. GLASS

6. BOTTLE

7. PLANT

8. COKE

Vocabulary

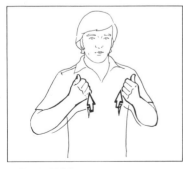

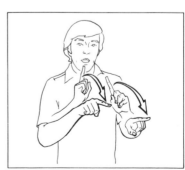

ADDRESS

AGAIN, repeat

ANSWER, respond

ASK

or palms together to chest

BABY

BICYCLE

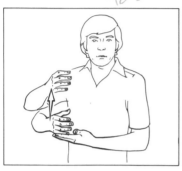

BOTTLE

BREAD

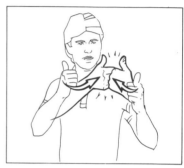

CHALLENGE, play against

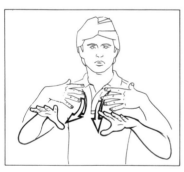

CLOTHES, DRESS, wear

thumbs stay on chest

COFFEE

COKE

DEPEND

(fingers stay together) bounce

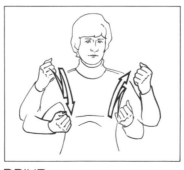

DRIVE

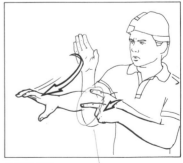

FORCE

pointer touching wrist

72

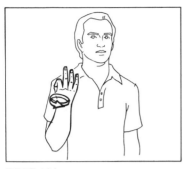

FRIDAY

FUNNY, amusing

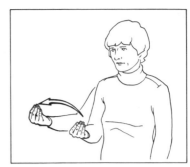

GIVE

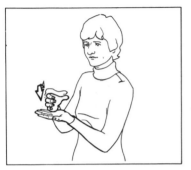

GLASS, CAN, cup

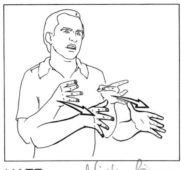

HATE *flick finger*

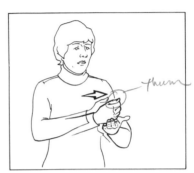

HELP, aid *thumb*

windows = tap teeth w/ pointer

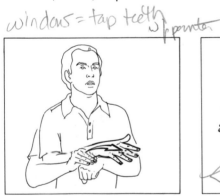

INFLUENCE, affect

INFORM, notify, obey

INTRODUCE

to chest
she introduces me
w/ one hand
(w/ come)

LOOK-AT, WATCH

MEAT, steak */ grab hand*

MILK

73

shake = sideways fist

Shakespeare J + like toss dice

MONDAY

w/ "p"

PAY

imagine from forehead fingers out

PICTURE, photograph

PLANT, spring *drops to "p"*

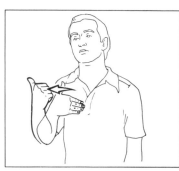

PREFER, rather *middle to chin*

PROUD, pride

REQUEST, ask

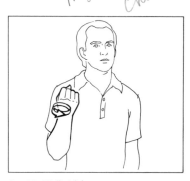

SATURDAY

SEND, mail to

Send object = flick fingers over back of hand

SHOW, demonstrate,
illustrate *(verb)*

SHY *(roll hand)*

keep p-fingers against cheek

prostitute=flick fingers
shame J + outward

SUGAR, sweet, cute

74

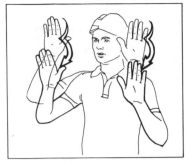

SUNDAY

SWEET

TEA

TELETYPEWRITER

TELL *or* "Speak"

THURSDAY

TICKET

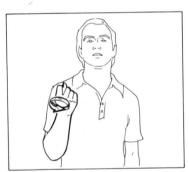

TUESDAY

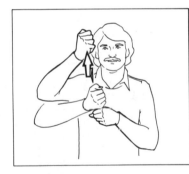

UMBRELLA

WAIT

WEDNESDAY

WRIST-WATCH

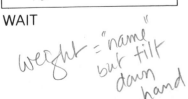

weight = "name" but tilt down hand

LESSON 7

Imperatives

Imperative sentences, or commands, are made in the following way:
1. The YOU pronoun is usually absent.
2. The signer looks directly at the person being commanded.
3. The verb has a sharp and tense movement. A sharp head nod may accompany the verb.

EXAMPLES:

A. WASH-DISH!   'Wash the dishes!'

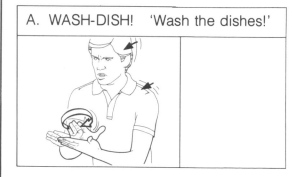

_____ t _____
B. TICKET YOU-GIVE-ME!   'Give me the ticket!'

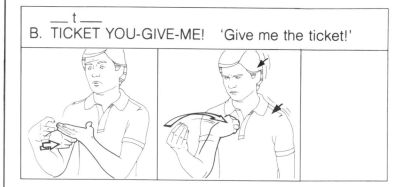

Some common imperatives are: STOP-IT, PAY-ATTENTION, COME-ON, GET-AWAY, GO-TO-IT.

C. I I-TELL-YOU FINISH, GO-TO-IT! WASH-DISH! 'I've told you—go and wash the dishes!'

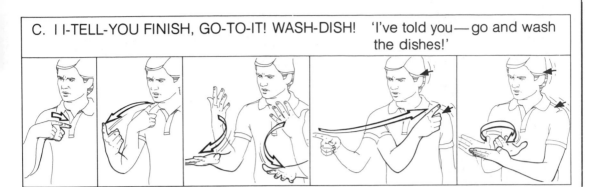

D. NOT LIKE I. STOP-IT! 'I don't like that. Stop it!'

or bounce side of hand + palm

NOTE: The YOU pronoun can be used at the beginning of the command for a more emphatic meaning.

E. <u>YOU</u> WASH-DISH! '<u>You</u> wash the dishes!'

more emphatic

Exercise 7.1:

Change the following sentences to commands.

EXAMPLE:

  __ t __
PICTURE YOU-SHOW-ME. 'You showed me the picture.'
   __ t __
  PICTURE YOU-SHOW ME! 'Show me the picture!'

1. TOMORROW YOU-GIVE-ME MONEY.

   __ t __
2. LETTER YOU-SEND-HER MOTHER.

  _ t _
3. T-T-Y YOU BUY YOU.

4. YOU PRACTICE SIGN YOU.

5. YOU REMEMBER SIGN YOU.

6. TOMORROW YOU AGAIN YOU-TELL-HER.

7. ADVERTISEMENT YOU-SEND-ME.

8. YOU PAY-ATTENTION YOU.

Using Numbers

1. When counting from 1 to 5 items as in 3 BOOK ('3 books') the palm faces inward to the signer. (The order BOOK 3 is also possible.)

EXAMPLE:

___ t ___
3 BOOK I HAVE.   'I have 3 books.'

I HAVE BOOK 3.   'I have 3 books.'
I HAVE 3 BOOK.   'I have 3 books.'

2. When indicating age, the sign OLD followed by a number is used. In this case the number is made with the palm facing outward.

EXAMPLE:

SISTER SHE OLD 3 SHE.   'My sister is 3 years old.'

(But not in the order: 3 OLD.)

3. When a number accompanies the sign TIME as in TIME 5 (to mean '5 o'clock'), the palm faces outward.

EXAMPLES:

A. BREAKFAST TIME 8. 'Breakfast is at 8 o'clock.'

or wiggle hand w/ number side to side 16 Turns

↳ slide off wrist to time

B. I WAIT UNTIL TIME 5, I GIVE-UP. 'I waited until 5 o'clock, then I gave up.'
(But not in the order: 3 TIME.)

Exercise 7.2:

Substitute the items given into the model sentence.

EXAMPLE:

I FIND 2 BOOK. 'I found 2 books.'
  CHAIR 4
  I FIND CHAIR 4. 'I found 4 chairs.'

1. 3 GLASS   3. 5 PENCIL   5. 4 KNIFE
2. COAT 1   4. STAMP 2   6. SPOON 3

EXAMPLE:

TOMORROW BROTHER OLD 3. 'Tomorrow my brother will be 3 years old.'
  OLD 7
  TOMORROW BROTHER OLD 7. 'Tomorrow my brother will be 7 years old.'

7. OLD 4   9. OLD 6   11. OLD 5
8. OLD 9   10. OLD 2   12. OLD 1

EXAMPLE:

FRIEND WILL SHE-MEET-ME TIME 2. 'My friend will meet me at 2 o'clock.'
  TIME 5
  FRIEND WILL SHE-MEET-ME TIME 5. 'My friend will meet me at 5 o'clock'

13. TIME 9   15. TIME 4   17. TIME 1
14. TIME 8   16. TIME 6   18. TIME 7

Personal Pronouns Incorporating Number

1. There are other forms of personal pronouns that incorporate number:

TWO-OF-US 'the two of us (we)'	TWO-OF-YOU 'the two of you (you, pl.'

TWO-OF-THEM 'the two of them (they)'

EXAMPLE:

TWO-OF-THEM SISTER.   'They (the two of them) are sisters.'

2. The numbers 3, 4, and 5 can be incorporated also:

FOUR-OF-US 'the four of us'	THREE-OF-YOU 'the three of you'

FIVE-OF-THEM 'the five of them'

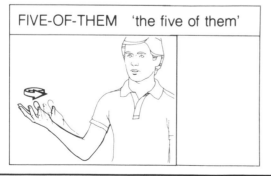

Exercise 7.3:

Substitute the following number-incorporating pronouns into the sentence given.

EXAMPLE:

TWO-OF-US PLAN GO-AWAY.   'We (the two of us) plan to go.'
   FOUR-OF-US
      FOUR-OF-US PLAN GO-AWAY.   'We (the four of us) plan to go.'

1. THREE-OF-US
2. FIVE-OF-US

3. TWO-OF-YOU
4. FOUR-OF-US

EXAMPLE:

THREE-OF-US GO-WITH WILL.   'We (the three of us) will go together.'

5. FIVE-OF-THEM
6. FOUR-OF-US

7. TWO-OF-THEM
8. THREE-OF-YOU

Plurals

There are several ways to make plurals. Two are shown below.

1. Add a number before or after the noun.

EXAMPLE:

I HAVE BOOK 3 I.   'I have 3 books.'

I HAVE 3 BOOK I.   'I have 3 books.'

81

2. Add a quantifier such as MANY, A-FEW, or SEVERAL before or after the noun.

EXAMPLE:

I HAVE BOOK MANY I.   'I have many books.'

I HAVE MANY BOOK I.   'I have many books.'

Exercise 7.4:

Change the following nouns to plural nouns with the number or quantifier given.

EXAMPLE:

SHE BUY SHIRT SHE.   'She bought a shirt.'
  (5)
    SHE BUY 5 SHIRT SHE.   'She bought 5 shirts.'
    SHE BUY SHIRT 5 SHE.   'She bought 5 shirts.'

1. HE GROW-UP RABBIT HE.   (10)

2. SON HE NEED PANTS HE.   (MANY)

3. SHE ORDER HAMBURGER SHE.   (2)

4. I ORDER FRENCH-FRIES I.   (3)

5. IT STORE HAVE SHOES IT.   (MANY)

6. STUDENT HE HAVE MISTAKE HE.   (A-FEW)

7. SHE FINISH SHE-GIVE-ME PICTURE.   (SEVERAL)

8. I FINISH I-MEET-HER NEW NEIGHBOR.   (SEVERAL)

                  n
9. TWO-OF-THEM NOT HAVE FRIEND.   (MANY)

10. PEOPLE STILL WAIT.   (A-FEW)

Vocabulary

ADVERTISEMENT,
publicize, propaganda

A-FEW

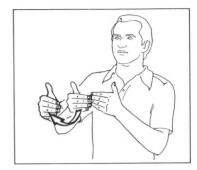

AFTER, from now on

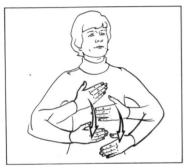

BODY

BOTH

BREAKFAST

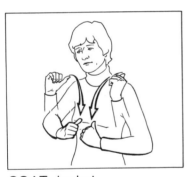

COAT, jacket

COME-ON

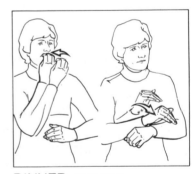

DINNER, supper

EYES

FACE

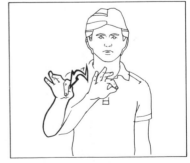

FRENCH-FRIES

83

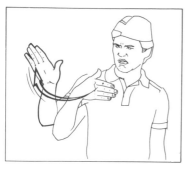

GET-AWAY

GO-TO-IT

GO-WITH, accompany

HAMBURGER

HANDS

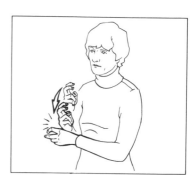

HARD

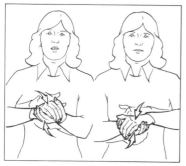

HEAD

HEART

KNIFE

LEFT, remaining

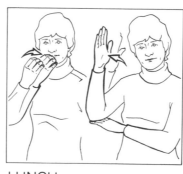

LUNCH

MANY, numerous

since/so far = roll wrists w/ pointer

while = scoop w/ pointers

after = palms ⊥ ; one to floor, other slides over

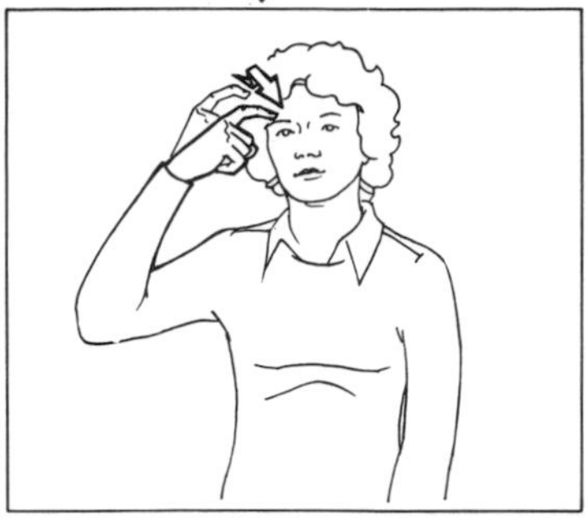

MIND

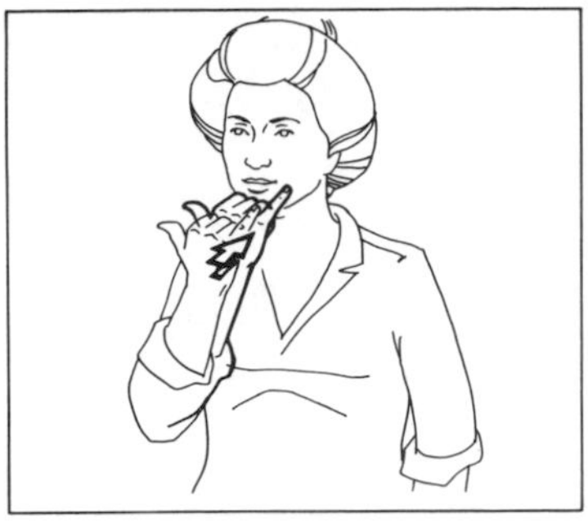

MISTAKE, error

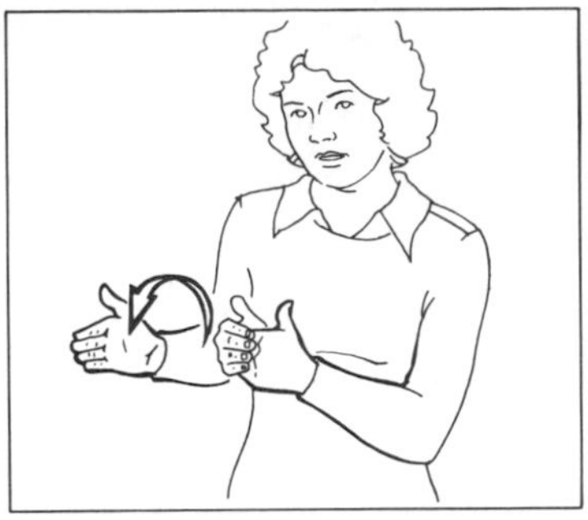

NEIGHBOR, next door

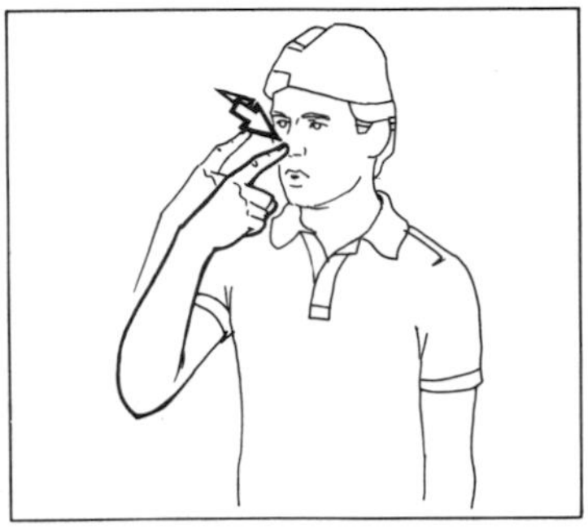

NOSE

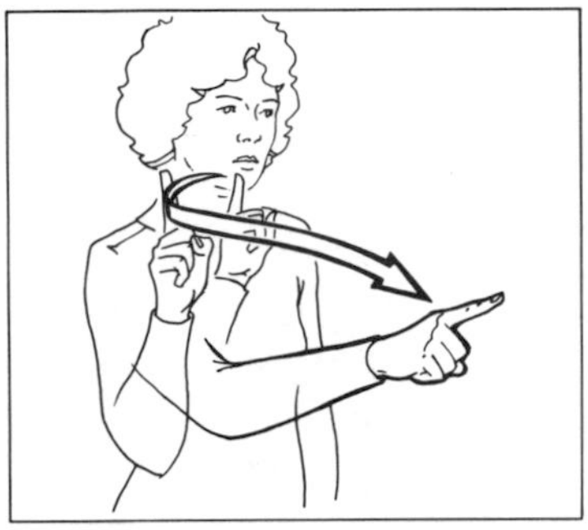

ORDER, command

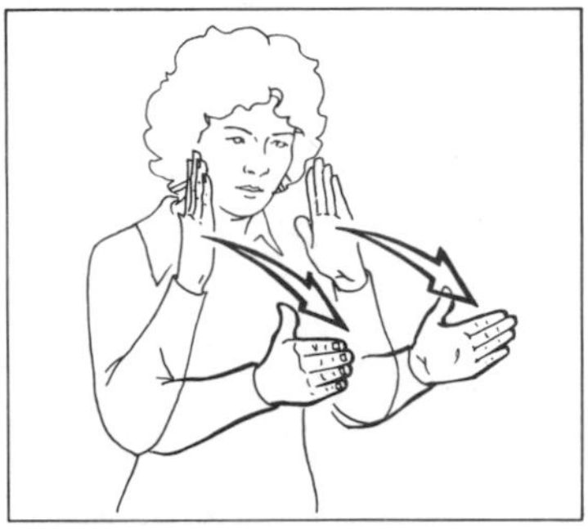

PAY-ATTENTION, concentrate

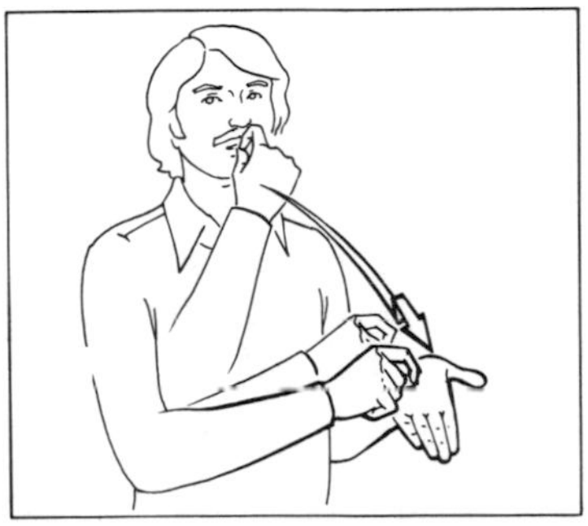

PENCIL

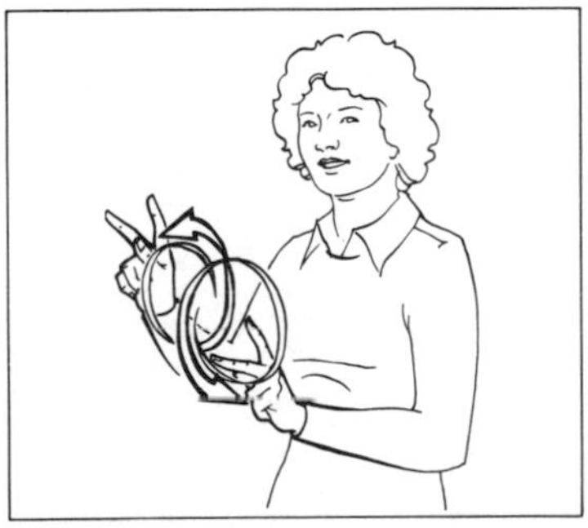

PEOPLE

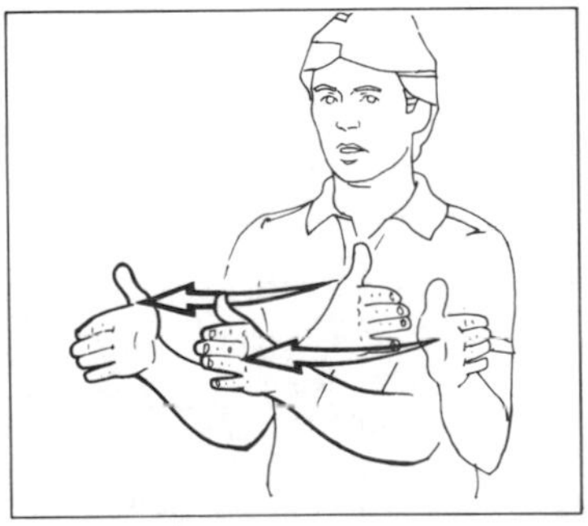

PLAN, prepare

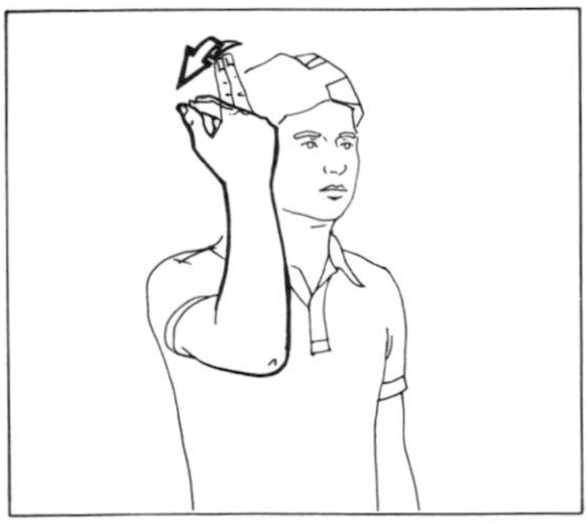

RABBIT

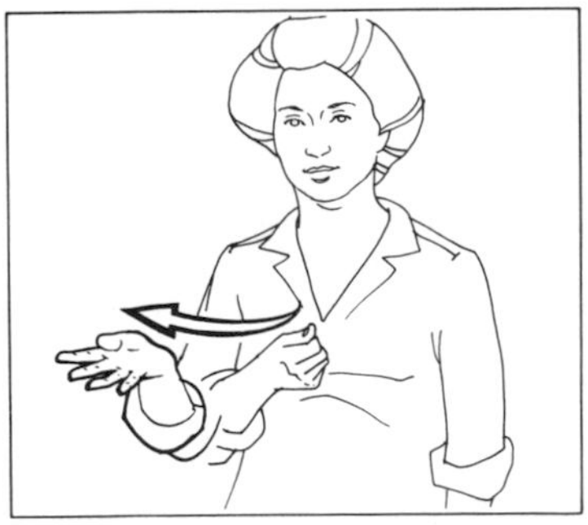

SEVERAL

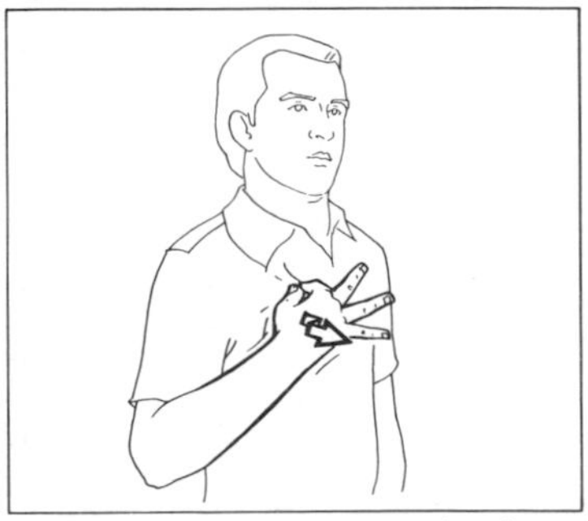

SHIRT

To = cross pointers ⊥

Decide = "if" pointer to forehead + downward ↓ (one motion)

SHOES

SOFT

SPOON, soup

STAMP, postage

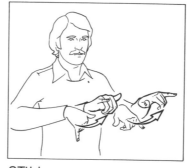

STILL

STOP-IT

STORE

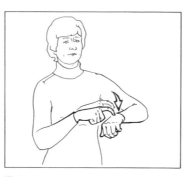

TIME

UNTIL, up to

WASH-DISH

DIALOGUE 2

Betty has just been introduced to Jack. Jack finds that she knows his brother. It is not unusual for deaf people who have never met before to have friends or acquaintances in common. This is due, largely, to many of them having attended state residential schools where children spend a great deal of their lives together. Visits to other schools for deaf children in neighboring states for sporting events or other civic events also contributes to meeting Deaf people from far away. Deaf people also attend events organized by the National Association of the Deaf, the American Athletic Association of the Deaf, and the World Recreation Association of the Deaf, which provide other opportunities for meeting other Deaf people.

Jack:
$$\underline{\hspace{3cm}}\ q\ \underline{\hspace{3cm}}$$
YOU KNOW MY BROTHER?

Betty:
$$\underline{\hspace{3cm}}\ y\ \underline{\hspace{3cm}}$$
YES. I FINISH I-MEET-HIM.   MY SISTER, YOUR BROTHER

TWO-THEM GOOD-FRIEND.

Jack:
$$\underline{\hspace{3cm}}\ n\ \underline{\hspace{3cm}}$$
I DON'T-KNOW YOUR SISTER DEAF.

Betty:
$$\underline{\hspace{2cm}}\ y\ \underline{\hspace{2cm}}$$
SHE DEAF SHE.   NAME SHE M-A-R-Y W-I-L-L-I-A-M-S.

Jack:
$$\underline{\hspace{2cm}}\ y\ \underline{\hspace{2cm}}$$
SURPRISED I.   I KNOW SHE.   BEFORE TIME I SEE SHE

LONG-AGO 6 YEAR.

Betty:
$$\underline{\hspace{2cm}}\ t\ \underline{\hspace{2cm}}$$
M-A-R-Y PICTURE, I HAVE MANY.   I I-CL:C↑-YOU WILL I.

Jack:
$$\underline{\hspace{2cm}}\ y\ \underline{\hspace{2cm}}$$
FINE.   I WANT SEE I.

already = flick fingers down

87

LESSON 8

WH-Questions

WH-questions ask for specific information. These questions use signs such as WHO, WHAT, WHEN, WHERE, WHY, WHICH, HOW, WHAT-FOR ('why'), HOW-MANY/HOW-MUCH. They are made by:
1. Squeezing the eyebrows together.
2. Moving the head slightly forward.
3. Looking directly at the person being asked the question.
_____ whq _____ will be used to represent the above grammatical features of WH-questions. WH-questions use the following form:

_____ whq _____
YOUR CAR WHERE?   'Where is your car?'

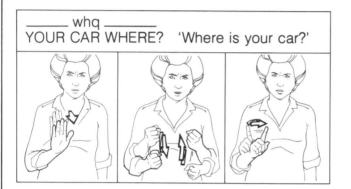

_____ whq _____
ICE-CREAM YOU WANT WHICH?   'Which (flavor of) ice cream do you want?'

MUST USE EXPRESSIONS

Exercise 8.1:

Form WH-questions using the statements given.

EXAMPLE:

MAN BUY NEW CAR HE.   'The man bought a new car.'
  WHO
      _____ whq _____
    BUY NEW CAR WHO?   'Who bought a new car?'
  WHAT
      _____ whq _____
    MAN BUY WHAT?   'What did the man buy?'

1. T-T-Y ARRIVE YESTERDAY.
   WHAT:
   WHEN:

2. AUNT LOSE SUITCASE.
   WHO:
   WHAT:
   WHEN:
   WHICH:

3. WIFE NOW SHE VISIT S-D SHE.
   WHO:
   WHERE:
   WHAT-FOR:
   WHY:

4. HORSE IT ESCAPE IT.
   HOW:
   WHEN:
   WHICH:

5. T-V BREAK LONG-AGO.
   WHEN:
   WHAT:
   HOW:

[handwritten notes: until = (drawing) with pointer]

[handwritten notes: Since = both hands roll wrists point out]

[handwritten notes: Either way = flip sideways "U" back-forth]

Other Forms of WH-Questions

Other forms of WH-questions are possible besides the form:
_____ whq _____
YOUR CAR WHERE?   'Where is your car?'
They are:

1. WH-sign at the beginning of the question:

EXAMPLES:

_____ whq _____
A. WHERE YOUR CAR?   'Where is your car?'

_____ whq _____
B. HOW YOU KNOW YOU?   'How do you know?'

2. WH-sign at the beginning and the end of the question:

EXAMPLES:

<u>_____ whq _____</u>
A. WHERE YOUR CAR WHERE?   'Where is your car?'

<u>_____ whq _____</u>
B. HOW YOU KNOW HOW?   'How do you know?'

3. The WH-marker can be used alone:

EXAMPLES:

<u>___ whq ___</u>
A. YOUR NAME?   'What is your name?'

<u>___ whq ___</u>
B. EXCUSE.   BATHROOM?   'Excuse me. Where is the bathroom?'

Exercise 8.2:

Form WH-questions from the statements in Exercise 8.1 using the forms:

<u>_____ whq ____</u>
WHO BUY NEW CAR?   'Who bought a new car?'
<u>_____ whq _____</u>
and WHO BUY NEW CAR WHO?   'Who bought a new car?'

90

The SELF Pronoun

The SELF pronoun has two functions:

1. It can function as a reflexive pronoun as shown in the following examples:

A. TO-TELEPHONE DOCTOR YOURSELF.   'You call the doctor yourself.'

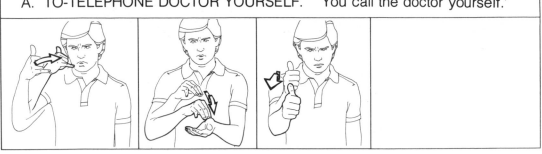

B. COOKIE I MAKE MYSELF.   'I made some cookies myself.'
C. CHILDREN WRITE LETTER THEMSELVES.   'The children wrote letters themselves.'

2. It can function as another form of personal pronoun as shown in the following examples:

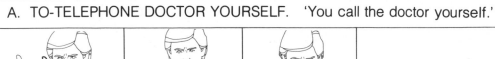

A. MYSELF TIRED, FEEL GOOD I.   'I am tired and don't feel well.'

B. HERSELF WANT BECOME DOCTOR SHE.   'She wants to become a doctor.'
C. THEMSELVES HAVE IDEA MANY.   'They have many ideas.'

They + thumb outward

pinkie "i,i" from forehead

press thumbs / palms twist/flip hands as

91

Exercise 8.3:

Answer the following questions with the appropriate reflexive pronoun.

EXAMPLE:

           _____ q _____
Question: YOU MAKE DRESS YOU?   'Did you make the dress?'

           _____ y _____
Response: YES, I MAKE MYSELF.   'Yes, I made it myself.'

        _____ q _____
1. PICTURE IT YOUR DAUGHTER DRAW?

        _____ q _____
2. YOU YOU-TELL-HIM YOU?

        _____ q _____
3. HOUSE YOU CLEAN-UP YOU?

        _____ q _____
4. THEY DECIDE WRITE LETTER?

        _____ q _____
5. BOOK HE WRITE HE?

        _____ q _____
6. HOUSE YOUR FATHER BUILD?

        _____ q _____
7. FLOWER YOU GROW YOU?

        _____ q _____
8. CAR IT BOY WASH HE?

Exercise 8.4:

Substitute the SELF personal pronoun for the personal pronouns in the following sentences.

EXAMPLE:

  __ t __
COLLEGE SHE WANT GO-AWAY.   'She wants to go to college.'

   __ t __
  COLLEGE HERSELF WANT GO-AWAY.   'She wants to go to college.'

```
         t         n
1.  TYPEWRITER I NOT HAVE.

2.  HE LONELY HE.

3.  SHE HAVE SKILL.

                 n
4.  THEY ENTHUSIASTIC STUDY NOT.

           q
5.  TEST YOU WORRY YOU?

             q
6.  ANY QUESTION YOU HAVE?
```

Vocabulary

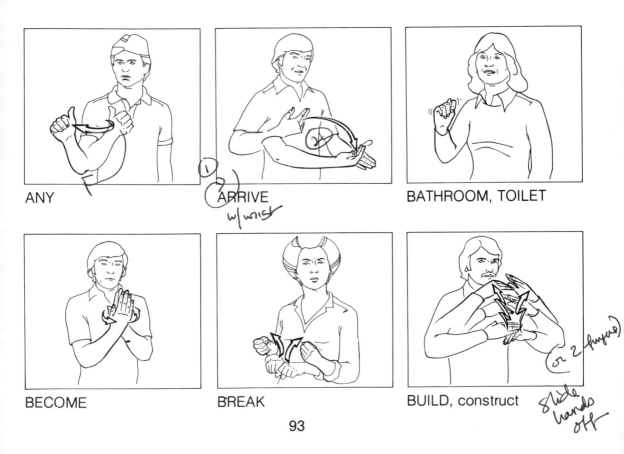

ANY   ARRIVE   BATHROOM, TOILET
                   w/ wrist

BECOME   BREAK   BUILD, construct

93

CANDY *sweet/sugar = 2 fingers*

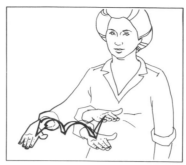

CHILDREN

CLEAN-UP

DECIDE, determined, decision

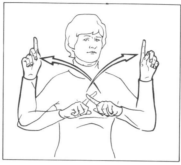

DIFFERENT

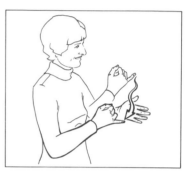

DRAW *Art too*

ENTHUSIASTIC *+ eager motivation*

(flick)

ESCAPE, run away, get away *sprint*

EXCUSE

FLOWER *nose = up^*

GROW

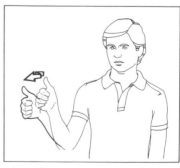

HIMSELF, HERSELF, ITSELF

94

paint = brush fingers against palm

HORSE

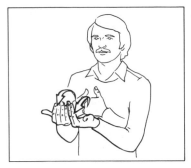

HOW

HOW-MANY, HOW-MUCH

ICE-CREAM

IDEA

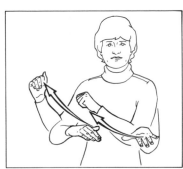

LEAVE, depart

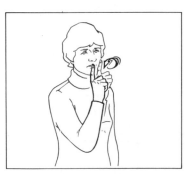

LONELY, lonesome

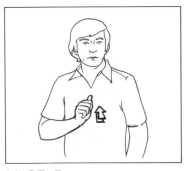

MYSELF

OURSELVES

QUESTION

SKILL, ability, expert

or 2 fingers
& flick

STUDY

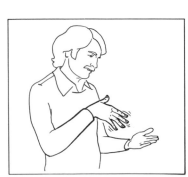

95

LOOK SEARCH cup hand C around face

 SUITCASE, purse w/ ("on" handle)

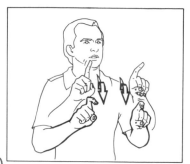 TEST, exam, quiz

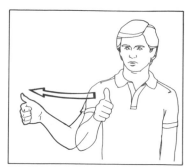 THEMSELVES

 TYPEWRITER

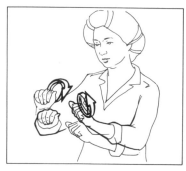 WASH

 WASH-FACE

 WASH-IN-MACHINE

 WHAT

 WHAT, where

 WHAT-FOR, why

 WHAT-TO-DO
(what are you doing?)

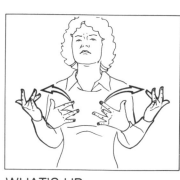 WHAT'S-UP

96

what'd ya do?
(or) what do you want me to do = touch chest

WHEN

to the shore

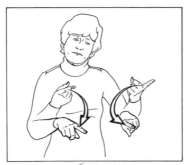

WHEN

" *happen*

WHERE

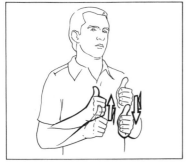

WHICH, or

WHO

WHO

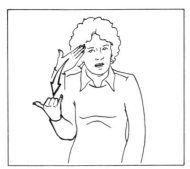

WHY

WORRY, concerned

trouble = flap hands 🖐🖐

YOURSELF

YOURSELVES

97

LESSON 19

Noun-Verb Pairs

There are many nouns and verbs which are related to each other in meaning and form and differ only in movement. These are called noun-verb pairs. Some verbs have a single movement and the related noun has a smaller, repeated movement.

EXAMPLE:

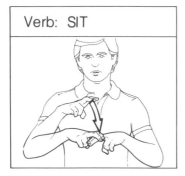

Verb: SIT

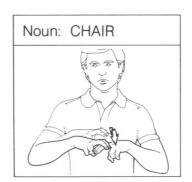

Noun: CHAIR

Other verbs have repeated movement and the related noun has a smaller, repeated movement.

EXAMPLE:

Verb: COMB-HAIR

Noun: COMB

Typical = two pointers bump fists one on top of other

Note that while verbs may vary in movement, the related nouns are smaller and repeated in movement. Some examples of noun-verb pairs are:

FLY - AIRPLANE   GO-BY-BOAT - BOAT

OPEN-DOOR - DOOR   GO-BY-TRAIN - TRAIN

OPEN-WINDOW - WINDOW   OPEN-BOOK - BOOK

MEET - MEETING	PUT-IN-GAS - GAS
GIVE-TICKET - TICKET	PUT-ON-HEARING-AID - HEARING-AID
LOCK-KEY	TO-TELEPHONE - TELEPHONE
TELL-STORY - STORY	TO-BICYCLE - BICYCLE
TYPE - TYPEWRITER	GROW - PLANT

Exercise 9.1:

Change the verb forms given in the questions below to their related noun forms in your answers.

EXAMPLE:

<u>   q   </u>
Question: YOU WANT SIT YOU? 'Do you want to sit down?'

<u>   y </u>
YES, I WANT . . .
<u>   y   </u>
Response: YES, I WANT CHAIR I. 'Yes, I want a chair.'

<u>   q   </u>
1. COP GIVE-TICKET HE?

<u>   y   </u>
COP SHE-GIVE-HIM . . .

<u>   q   </u>
2. WE MEET TOMORROW?

<u>   y   </u>
YES, TOMORROW TIME 3 HAVE . . .

<u>   q   </u>
3. YOU ENJOY TO-BICYCLE?

<u>   y   </u>
YES, I HAVE NEW . . .

<u>   q   </u>
4. YOU FINISH PUT-IN-GAS TODAY?

<u> n </u>
NO, I NEED . . .

<u>   q   </u>
5. I SEE YOU PUT-ON-HEARING-AID?

<u> y </u>
I HAVE . . .

<u>   whq   </u>
6. TIME I TO-TELEPHONE YOU
<u>   </u>
TOMORROW?

<u>   n   </u>
NOT TO-TELEPHONE . . . BREAK.

<u>   q   </u>
7. YOU KNOW HOW TYPE?

<u>   y   </u>
YES, I HAVE . . .

8. _____q_____
   DOOR YOU FINISH LOCK?

_____n_____
I NOT HAVE . . .

9. OPEN-BOOK NOW!

_____n_____
I NOT HAVE . . .

10. _____whq_____
    YOU FLY, GO-BY-TRAIN, WHICH?

I WANT . . .

Using Subject as Topic

The topic marker may be used on subjects as well as objects. The marker is used to specify, and in some cases emphasize, the subject.

EXAMPLES:

____t____
A. BICYCLE MY BREAK.   'My bicycle, it's broken.'

__t__
B. HE KID FALL HE.   'The kid, he fell.'

____t___
C. DEAF THEY MEET TOMORROW.   'Deaf people, they are meeting tomorrow.'

Exercise 9.2:

Use topic marking with the subjects in the following sentences.

EXAMPLE:

WIFE HAVE NEW WORK.   'My wife has a new job.'

_t_
WIFE HAVE NEW WORK.   'My wife, she has a new job.'

1. GIRLFRIEND HAVE BLOND HAIR.

2. CALIFORNIA WOW NICE.

3. TEACHER SHE-BAWL-OUT-HIM.

4. RAIN STOP.

5. LEADER SHE-ASK-ME QUESTION.

6. HIS WRIST-WATCH STEAL.

_____ n _____
7. TREE IT NOT LOOK GOOD.

8. PERFORMANCE WONDERFUL.

9. PLANT NEED WATER.

10. MEETING CANCEL.

Vocabulary

ACT, perform
Noun: PERFORMANCE

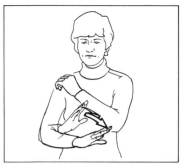

AUTUMN, Fall

BAWL-OUT

BLOND

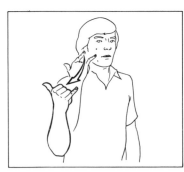

CALIFORNIA, gold

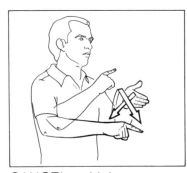

CANCEL, criticize,
correct

COMB-HAIR
Noun: COMB

COP, POLICE

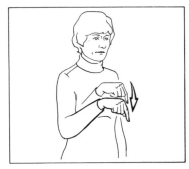

DOWN

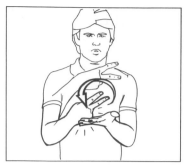

FALL, FALL-DOWN

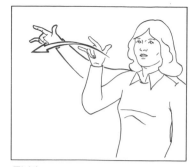

FLY
Noun: AIRPLANE,
AIRPORT

GIVE-TICKET
Noun: TICKET

GO-BY-BOAT
Noun: BOAT

GO-BY-TRAIN
Noun: TRAIN

HAIR

KID

LEAD, guide

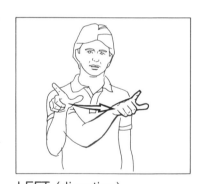

LEFT (direction)

 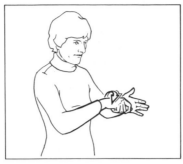 

LIBRARY

LOCK
Noun: KEY

LOOK, appearance

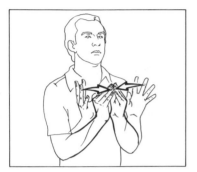 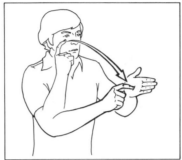 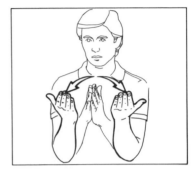

MEET (group)
Noun: MEETING,
convention

NOTICE, recognize

OPEN-BOOK
Noun: BOOK

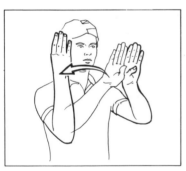  

OPEN-DOOR
Noun: DOOR

OPEN-WINDOW
Noun: WINDOW

PERSON

 PLACE

 PUT-IN-GAS
Noun: GAS

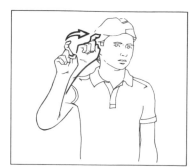 PUT-ON-HEARING-AID
Noun: HEARING-AID

 PUT-ON-RING
Noun: RING

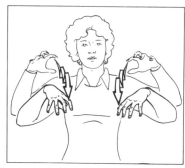 RAIN

 RIGHT (direction)

 SIT
Noun: CHAIR, seat

 STEAL

 STOP

 SUMMER

 TELL-STORY
Noun: STORY

 THING

TO-BICYCLE
Noun: BICYCLE

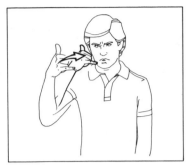

TO-TELEPHONE
Noun: TELEPHONE

TREE

TYPE
Noun: TYPEWRITER

UP

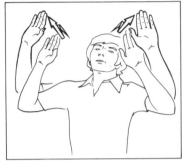

WONDERFUL, fantastic,
great

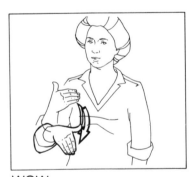

WOW

Basic Sentence Structure: Using Modals

The modals that can accompany other verbs in a sentence are: CAN, SHOULD, MUST, WILL, FINISH, MAYBE. There are three types of sentence structure with modals.

1. The modal is at the end of the sentence:

EXAMPLE:

```
_____ t _____
```
TELEPHONE NUMBER WOMAN SHE-GIVE-ME. SHOULD SHE.
'The woman should give me the telephone number.'

2. The modal precedes the verb:

EXAMPLE:

```
_____ t _____
```
TELEPHONE NUMBER WOMAN SHOULD SHE-GIVE-ME SHE.
'The woman should give me the telephone number.'

3. The modal both precedes the verb and is repeated at the end of the sentence:

EXAMPLE:

```
_____ t _____
```
TELEPHONE NUMBER WOMAN SHOULD SHE-GIVE-ME SHOULD SHE.
'The woman should give me the telephone number.'

Exercise 10.1:

Use the modal given at the end of the following sentences.

EXAMPLE:

I LECTURE TIME 3 I.   'I lecture at 3 o'clock.'
  (CAN)
      I LECTURE TIME 3 CAN I.   'I can lecture at 3 o'clock.'

1. SHE SEE DOCTOR SHE.   (SHOULD)

    ————— q —————
2. LETTER YOU GET YOU?   (FINISH)

3. TOMORROW PRESIDENT APPEAR.   (MAYBE)

4. HE RECOVER HE.   (WILL)

5. I WIN RACE I.   (MUST)

6. I LIPREAD.   (CAN)

7. LETTER I TYPE 1-MINUTE I.   (CAN)

8. S-F YOU VISIT YOU.   (MUST)

9. HE TAKE-UP MORE CLASS HE.   (SHOULD)

10. SISTER MARRY.   (WILL)

Exercise 10.2:

Do Exercise 10.1 above with the modal preceding the verb.

EXAMPLE:

I LECTURE TIME 3 I.   'I lecture at 3 o'clock.'

  (CAN)
      I CAN LECTURE TIME 3 I.   'I can lecture at 3 o'clock.'

Using Negative Modals

Some negative modals are: CAN'T, NOT-YET, REFUSE.

EXAMPLES:

A. $\overline{\text{I DANCE}\underset{n}{}\text{CAN'T I.}}$ 'I can't dance.'

I DANCE CAN'T I.   'I can't dance.'

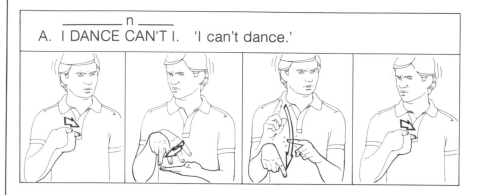

B. I EAT NOT-YET.   'I haven't eaten.'

C. I I-TELL-YOU REFUSE I.   'I won't tell you.'

Exercise 10.3:

Substitute negative modals for the modals in the sentences given.

EXAMPLE:

I COLLECT MONEY FINISH I.   'I have collected the money.'
        n
I COLLECT MONEY NOT-YET I.   'I haven't collected the money.'

1. I STAY 1-HOUR CAN I.

2. HE ACCEPT RESPONSIBILITY WILL HE.

3. HE FINISH COOK FOOD HE.

4. I GET-UP TIME 6 CAN I.

        t
5. TELEPHONE NUMBER HE MEMORIZE FINISH HE.

6. SHE BORN BABY FINISH SHE.

7. MAN HE HE-PAY-ME WILL HE.

8. $\overline{\text{LETTER}}^{\_\_t\_\_}$ HE-SEND-ME FINISH HE.

9. I FINISH TRY ESTABLISH C-L-U-B I.

10. ADDRESS SHE PUT-DOWN FOR-YOU CAN SHE.

Using Modals as Responses to Yes/No Questions

The modals can be used as responses to Yes/No questions in the following forms:

Questions:

$\overline{\text{YOU DRIVE}}^{_____q_____}\text{CAN YOU?}$
'Can you drive?'

Responses

$\overline{\text{I CAN I.}}^{\_\_y\_\_}$ 'Yes, I can.'

$\overline{\text{I CAN'T I.}}^{\_\_\_n\_\_}$ 'No, I can't.'

$\overline{\text{I BUY BOOK SHOULD I?}}^{_____q_____}$
'Should I buy the book?'

$\overline{\text{YES, YOU SHOULD YOU.}}^{_____y_____}$
'Yes, you should.'

$\overline{\text{I PAY MUST I?}}^{\_\_\_q\_\_\_}$
'Do I have to pay?'

$\overline{\text{YES, YOU MUST YOU.}}^{\_\_\_\_\_y\_\_\_\_\_}$
'Yes, you have to.'

‾‾‾q‾‾‾
I PASS WILL I?
'Will I pass?'

‾‾‾‾‾‾q‾‾‾‾‾‾
YOU WORK WILL YOU?
'Will you work?'

‾‾‾‾‾‾‾q‾‾‾‾‾‾‾
MEAT YOU COOK FINISH YOU?
'Have you cooked the meat?'

‾‾‾‾‾q‾‾‾‾‾
HE PASS MAYBE HE?
'He may pass?'

‾‾‾‾y‾‾‾‾
YOU WILL YOU.
'Yes, you will.'

‾‾‾y‾‾‾
YES, I WILL I.
'Yes, I will.'

‾‾‾‾n‾‾‾‾
NO, I REFUSE I.
'No, I won't.'

‾‾y‾‾
I FINISH I.
'Yes, I have.'

‾‾‾n‾‾‾
I NOT-YET I.
'No, I haven't.'

‾‾‾‾y‾‾‾‾
YES, HE MAYBE HE.
'Yes, he may.'

Exercise 10.4:

Form appropriate responses to the following questions.

Example:

‾‾‾‾‾‾‾q‾‾‾‾‾‾
Question: YOU WORK WILL YOU?   'Will you work?'
YES . . .

‾‾‾y‾‾‾
Response: YES I WILL I.   'Yes, I will.'

Question	**Response**
‾‾‾‾‾q‾‾‾‾‾ 1. YOU-HELP-ME CAN YOU?	NO . . .
‾‾‾‾‾‾‾q‾‾‾‾‾‾ 2. SHE SLEEP NOW SHOULD SHE?	YES . . .
‾‾‾‾‾‾q‾‾‾‾‾ 3. CAR YOU BUY MAYBE YOU?	YES . . .
‾‾‾‾‾‾‾q‾‾‾‾‾‾ 4. AGAIN TO-TELEPHONE YOU CAN I?	YES . . .
‾‾‾‾‾‾‾q‾‾‾‾‾‾‾ 5. RESTAURANT HE FINISH ESTABLISH HE?	NO . . .
‾‾‾‾‾‾q‾‾‾‾‾ 6. POLICE CATCH MAN FINISH?	YES . . .
‾‾‾‾‾q‾‾‾‾‾ 7. PARTY I PLAN SHOULD I?	YES . . .
‾‾‾‾‾q‾‾‾‾‾ 8. RACE HE MAYBE WIN HE?	YES . . .
‾‾‾‾‾‾‾‾q‾‾‾‾‾‾‾‾ 9. TEST TOMORROW SHE TAKE-UP WILL SHE?	YES . . .

Vocabulary

ACCEPT

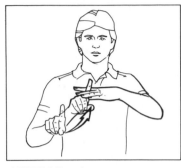

APPEAR, show up

BAKE, oven

BETWEEN

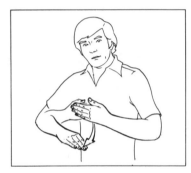

BORN, birth

CAN

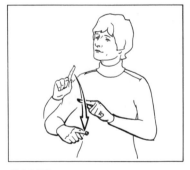

CAN'T

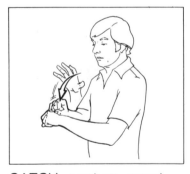

CATCH, capture, arrest

COLLECT

COMPETE
Noun: RACE, SPORTS,
competition, contest

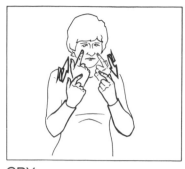

CRY

DIVORCE

ENGAGEMENT

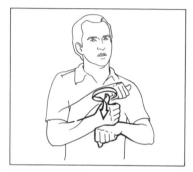

ESTABLISH, set up,
found

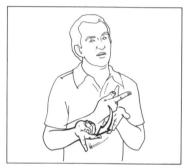

FAIL

FAST

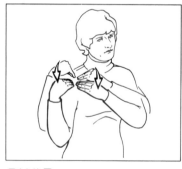

FAULT,
RESPONSIBILITY,
burden

FLUNK

 GET, receive, obtain

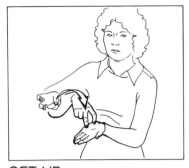 GET-UP

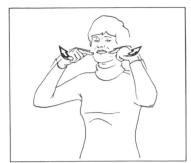 LAUGH

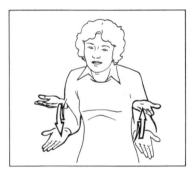 LECTURE, speech, presentation

 LIPREAD, oral, speech

 MARRY, marriage

 MAYBE, might

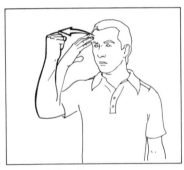 MEMORIZE

 MORE, further

 MOST

 MUST, have to

 NOT-YET

113

NUMBER

PARTY

PASS

PRESIDENT,
superintendent

PROTECT, guard, defend

PUT-DOWN, write down,
record

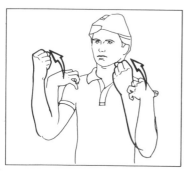

RECOVER, get well

REFUSE, won't

RESTAURANT

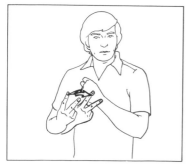

SAVE, preserve

SHOULD

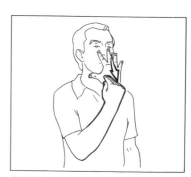

SLEEP

114

SLOW

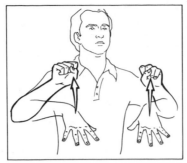

TAKE-UP

THINK

TRY, attempt, effort

WEDDING

WIN

NOTES

DIALOGUE 3

Jack is telling Tom about a film made by the National Association of the Deaf in 1913. This film is part of a series of performances, lectures, sermons, and parables produced by the NAD for the purpose of preserving signing for future generations. In fact, the Veditz lecture referred to here is called "The Preservation of the Sign Language." These films, especially the Veditz film, strike a chord among Deaf people of today because of the long history of attempts to ban, alter, or denigrate American Sign Language.

Jack: I RECENTLY SEE MOVIE INTERESTING. ITSELF OLD MOVIE,

SIGN LECTURE B-Y G-E-O-R-G-E V-E-D-I-T-Z. YOU SEE FINISH

YOU?

    ____ n ___   _____ whq _____

Tom: NOT-YET I. V-E-D-I-T-Z WHO?

Jack: HIMSELF DEAF, PRESIDENT N-A-D LONG-AGO 1913.

   ___t ___

SIGN HIS CAN NOTICE OLD, DIFFERENT.

    _____ whq _____

Tom: MAKE MOVIE WHAT FOR?

Jack: N-A-D FINISH COLLECT 5,000 DOLLAR, MAKE MOVIE. IT

WANT SAVE, PROTECT SIGN FOR FUTURE DEAF.

    __ whq _

Tom: I WANT SEE MOVIE. WHERE?

Jack: LIBRARY HAVE SHOULD. YOU-ASK-IT LIBRARY.

LESSON 11

Adverbials of Place: HERE and THERE

In addition to indicating pronominals, pointing is also used as adverbials of place, such as HERE and THERE.

HERE₁	HERE₂	THERE

The direction of the point for THERE is in the actual direction of the referent.

EXAMPLES:

A. MY HOME HERE. 'My home is here.'

B. MY HOME THERE. 'My home is over there.'

118

Exercise 11.1:

Use the following signs in sentences with HERE or THERE. Remember to point in the direction of the referent for THERE.

EXAMPLE:

MY CLASS
    MY CLASS HERE.   'My class is here.'

1. MY HOME

2. YOUR GLASSES

3. CAR

4. COKE MACHINE

5. WOMAN

6. STORE

7. BASEBALL GAME

8. CHURCH OLD

9. PAPER

10. YOUR FRIEND

NOTE: Use of THIS/THAT

1. The sign THIS/THAT can be used as a demonstrative to identify a noun. The location of THIS/THAT is the same as the location of the noun.

EXAMPLES:

_____ t _____
A. THAT BICYCLE WOW EXPENSIVE.   'That bicycle there is really expensive.'

B. THIS BICYCLE 'This bicycle here'	C. THAT BICYCLE 'That bicycle there'

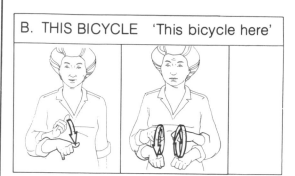 

2. Another related sign: THAT-ONE is usually followed by the pronoun showing the location of the referent.

EXAMPLES:

—————————— q ——————————
A. REMEMBER WOMAN I EXPLAIN, THAT-ONE SHE.   'Remember I explained about the woman? Well, that's her.'

—————————————— q ——————————————
B. THAT-ONE YOU GOOD-FRIEND MY BROTHER YOU?
'Are you the one that's a good friend of my brother?'

Verbs Incorporating Location

Some verbs change their movement to indicate a change from one location to another. Some of these verbs are:

GO	COME	DRIVE
MOVE	WALK	PUT
BRING	FLY	RUN

EXAMPLES:

To there:

__ t ___
A. FRIEND I GO-THERE VISIT.   'I went to visit my friend.'

B. BEFORE AUTUMN, BOSS MOVE-THERE CHICAGO.   'My boss moved to Chicago last fall.'

To here:

__ t ___
C. FRIEND COME-HERE VISIT.   'My friend came to visit me.'

D. I URGE FRIEND MOVE-HERE S-D.   'I persuaded my friend to move here to San Diego.'

From there to there:

__ t ___
E. FRIEND THERE-GO-THERE VISIT.   'My friend went there (from there) for a visit.'

Exercise 11.2:

Substitute the verbs in parentheses into the sentences given.

EXAMPLE:

BEFORE I GO-THERE I.   'I went there before.'
  (DRIVE)
        BEFORE I DRIVE-THERE I.   'I drove there before.'

1. BEFORE I DRIVE-THERE I.   (WALK)

2. BEFORE I DRIVE-THERE I.   (FLY)

3. FURNITURE HEAVY SHE BRING-THERE.   (MOVE)

4. BEFORE YOU COME-HERE YOU.   (DRIVE)

5. BEFORE YOU COME-HERE YOU.   (WALK)

6. BEFORE YOU COME-HERE YOU.   (FLY)

7. BOOK MANY SHE BRING-HERE.   (PUT)

8. CHICAGO, L-A HE THERE-MOVE-THERE HE.   (DRIVE)

9. CHICAGO, L-A HE THERE-MOVE-THERE HE.   (FLY)

10. STORE, YOUR HOME SHE THERE-WALK-THERE.   (DRIVE)

11. STORE, YOUR HOME SHE THERE-WALK-THERE.   (BRING)

FINISH as Conjunction

When used as a conjunction, FINISH is used like the English word, 'then.' It is often used to link sentences showing a sequence of events.

EXAMPLE:

I DRIVE-THERE BOX SEND FINISH, THERE-DRIVE-THERE FOOD STORE BUY FINISH, DRIVE-HERE HOME.   'I drove there, mailed a box, then drove to the food store to shop for food, then drove home.'

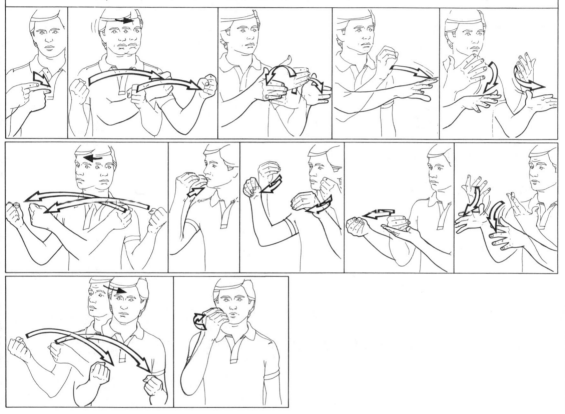

Exercise 11.3:

Combine the following sentences using FINISH as conjunction.

EXAMPLES:

MONEY I-SEND-HIM.   'I sent him the money.'
TICKET HE-SEND-ME.   'He sent me the ticket.'
  MONEY I-SEND-HIM FINISH TICKET HE-SEND-ME.
  'I sent him the money then he sent me the ticket.'

1. CHICAGO HE MOVE-THERE, STAY 2 YEAR.

   HE THERE-MOVE-THERE WASHINGTON.

2. C-F NOW I-GIVE-YOU.

   YOU-GIVE-HIM TOMORROW.

3. I STAY-HERE 1-WEEK WITH SISTER.

   I GO-THERE VISIT MOTHER.

4. BREAKFAST I COOK.

   YOU WASH-DISH.

5. SUITCASE I PACK.

   I GO-THERE AIRPORT.

6. PERFORMANCE PRACTICE ALL-DAY.

   TONIGHT HAVE PARTY THERE MY HOME.

Vocabulary

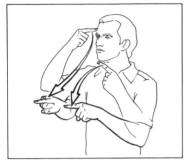

AGREE

ALL

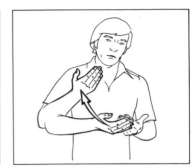

ALMOST

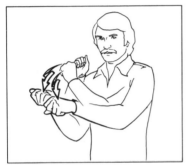

BASEBALL

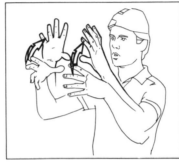

BASKETBALL

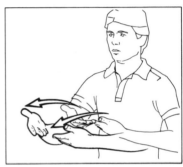

BRING, carry, deliver

CHAT, converse

CHICAGO

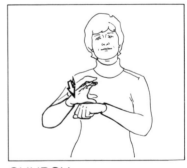

CHURCH

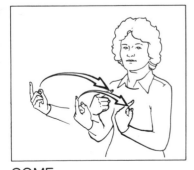

COME

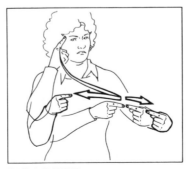

DISAGREE

DRIVE-TO

 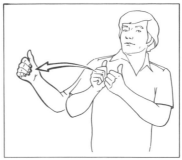 

EMPTY, bare, nude FAR, distant FOOTBALL

 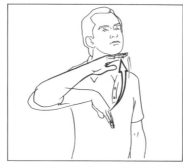 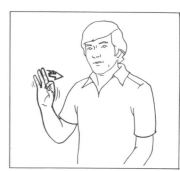

FULL, complete FULL, fed up FURNITURE

 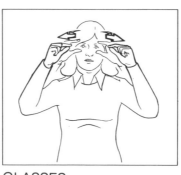 

GAME GLASSES GO

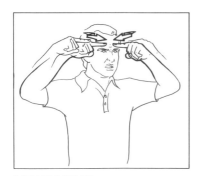  

HEADACHE HEAD-COLD, HERE
handkerchief

HERE

IMPORTANT, worth it, valuable

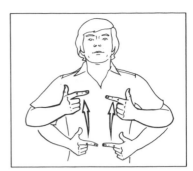

LIVE, life

MACHINE, engine, factory

MOVE-TO

NEAR, close

bring inside hand to outside

NEW-YORK

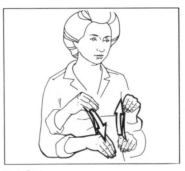

PACK

PHILADELPHIA

PUT

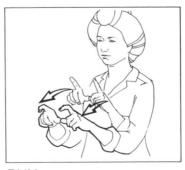

RUN

TALK, speak

CA = gold (mid finger → cheek) + curve "C"

TEMPLE

THAT

THAT-ONE

THERE, over there

THIS

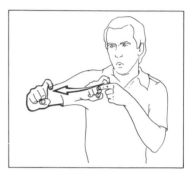

TO-TTY

URGE, persuade

WALK-TO

NOTES

LESSON 12

Existential HAVE

The sign HAVE has two meanings:
1. It indicates possession.

EXAMPLE:

I HAVE MONEY I.   'I have money.'

2. It indicates existence.

EXAMPLES:

A. IT KITCHEN HAVE MILK.   'There is milk in the kitchen.'

B. IT STORE HAVE FOOD IT.   'There is food in the store.'
C. IT HAVE PAPER IT.   'There is paper.'

Exercise 12.1:

Using signs from the following list, form existential HAVE sentences.

EXAMPLES:

A. HOME, COFFEE
   IT HOME HAVE COFFEE.   'There is coffee at home.'

B. RESTAURANT, WATER
   IT RESTAURANT HAVE WATER.   'There is water in the restaurant.'

1. RESTAURANT, FOOD

2. HOME, TEA

3. STORE, SHOES

4. SCHOOL, DEAF STUDENT

5. RESTAURANT, MEAT

6. KITCHEN, TABLE

7. HOUSE, CHAIR

8. RESTAURANT, RESTROOM

9. R-E-F, CREAM

10. BOOK, SIGN

Pronominal Classifiers

Some classifiers can be used as pronouns, that is, they can replace nouns. Three examples are:

CL:3	CL: ∧	CL:B
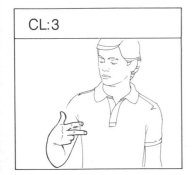	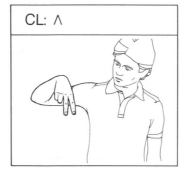	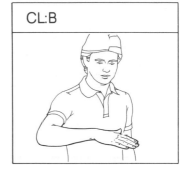

For vehicles such as a car, a bus, a bicycle, a truck.

For any person or two-legged animal such as a woman, a child, or a gorilla.

For any flat object such as a piece of paper, a magazine, a newspaper.

When used with nouns, these classifiers can show the location of the noun. The noun usually precedes the classifier in the sentence.

EXAMPLES:

_ t _
A. CAR CL:3-HERE.   'The car is near here.'

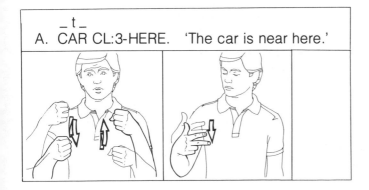

131

```
          _ t _
B.  CAR CL:3-THERE.    'The car is over there.'
```

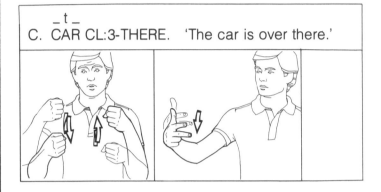

```
          _ t _
C.  CAR CL:3-THERE.    'The car is over there.'
```

Exercise 12.2:

Substitute the appropriate classifier for the HERE or THERE adverbials of place.

EXAMPLE:

I SEE YOUR V-A-N THERE.   'I see your van over there.'
   I SEE YOUR V-A-N CL:3-THERE.   'I see your van over there.'

1. WOMAN THERE, SHE-LOOK-AT-ME.

2. I ENTER, LETTER THERE.

3. SHOULD BICYCLE THERE.

4. SURPRISED ME.   PRESIDENT HERE.

    _____ t _____
5. CAR BLUE THERE, THAT-ONE HIS.

6. SHE FORGET LEFT MAGAZINE THERE.

7. RECENTLY BROTHER HERE, NOW GONE.

8. CAR THERE, NOW PUT-IN-GAS.

Locational Relationships

Pronominal classifiers can be used to show locational relationships such as "on," "under," "behind," "in front of," "beside," "facing each other," "on top of," etc.

EXAMPLES:

'two vehicles next to each other'

'two vehicles, one in front of the other'

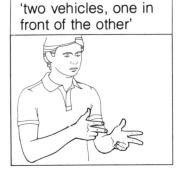

'two persons facing each other'

'one flat object on top of another'

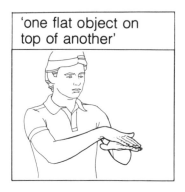

'a container on top of a flat surface'

'a container under a flat surface'

Exercise 12.3:

Using pronominal classifiers, indicate the locational relationship of the objects or persons in the following pictures. Use the model sentence given.

EXAMPLE:

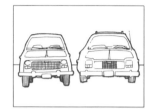

I SEE

    I SEE CAR CL:3-NEXT-TO-CL:3.   'I saw the two cars next to each other.'

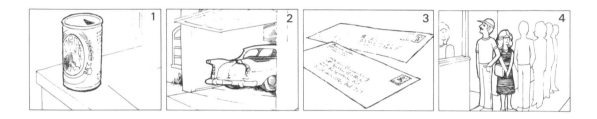

NOTE: Adding Movement to Pronominal Classifiers

The action of persons or objects can be indicated by adding movement to pronominal classifiers.

EXAMPLES:

'one vehicle passing another'	'two vehicles colliding head-on'
	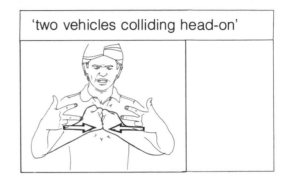

'a person diving off a platform'	'a container falling off a flat surface'
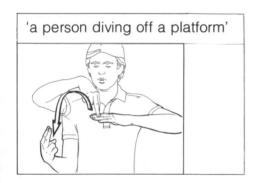	

Vocabulary

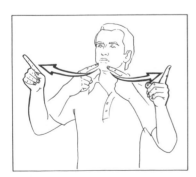

ANNOUNCE,
announcement

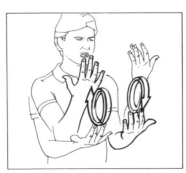

BURN, FIRE

CREAM

135

DISAPPOINT, miss

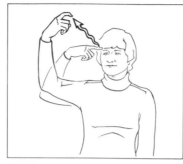

DREAM, daydream

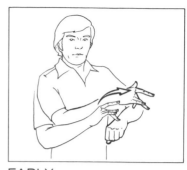

EARLY

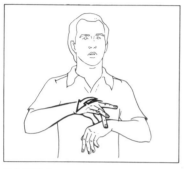

EARTH, geography

ENTER, go into

GONE

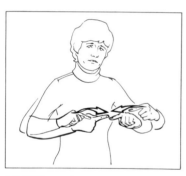

HURT, pain

KITCHEN

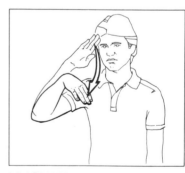

KNOW-THAT

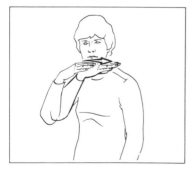

LIE

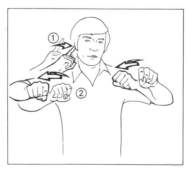

LOUD

LUCKY, delicious

136

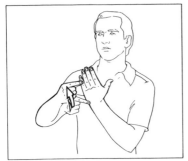

MAGAZINE, brochure, journal, booklet

MISS

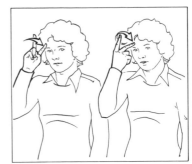

MISUNDERSTAND, misconception

MOON

NOISE, noisy

POOR, poverty

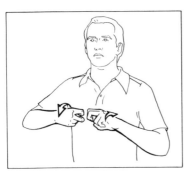

PROBLEM

PROMISE, commit, pledge, swear

QUIET, calm, peaceful

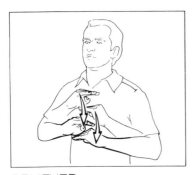

RELIEVED

REST

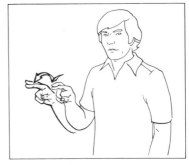

RESTROOM, bathroom

RICH, wealthy

SAME, like, alike

SAME, like, alike, similar

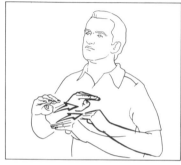
SATISFY, satisfied

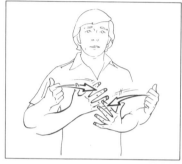
SCARE, frighten

STREET, road, way, path

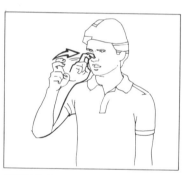
STRICT

SUN

SUNRISE

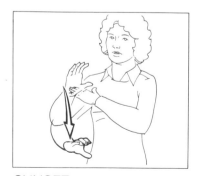
SUNSET

THIRSTY, thirst

VOICE, vocalize

138

WAKE-UP

WET, damp, moist

LESSON 13

Mass Quantifiers

The quantifiers SOME, A-LITTLE, and PLENTY are added either before a mass noun or at the end of the sentence.

EXAMPLES:

A. HAVE FURNITURE PLENTY I.   'I have a lot of furniture.'

HAVE PLENTY FURNITURE I.   'I have a lot of furniture.'

B. I THINK HAVE LEFT FOOD SOME.   'I think there's some food left.'

I THINK HAVE LEFT SOME FOOD.   'I think there's some food left.'

C. I EAT CHEESE A-LITTLE.   'I'll eat a little cheese.'
I EAT A-LITTLE CHEESE.   'I'll eat a little cheese.'

Exercise 13.1:

Substitute the following mass quantifiers into the sentences given.

EXAMPLE:

I PLENTY WORK LEFT.   'I have a lot of work left (to do)'.
  (A-LITTLE)
    I A-LITTLE WORK LEFT.   'I have a little work left (to do).'

1. HE CRAZY-FOR CHEESE, HAVE SOME I.   (PLENTY)

2. $\overline{\underline{\quad\quad} \text{ t } \underline{\quad\quad}}$
   SPORTS THING RESIDENTIAL-SCHOOL HAVE PLENTY.   (SOME)

3. $\overline{\underline{\;} \text{ t } \underline{\;}}$
   WATER CALIFORNIA NOW HAVE A-LITTLE.   (PLENTY)

4. $\overline{\underline{} \text{ t } \underline{}}$
   MEAT IT HAVE LEFT IT SOME.   (A-LITTLE)

5. $\overline{\underline{\quad} \text{ t } \underline{\;}}$
   YOUR PIE GRANDMOTHER WANT A-LITTLE.   (SOME)

More on Quantifiers

Some classifiers also serve as quantifiers. The classifiers below are used to indicate:
1. the amount of liquid,
2. the thickness of a solid,
3. the height of a stack.
They are:

CL:G	CL:Ḷ	CL:BB↑↓

EXAMPLES:

A. MUST I READ CL:BB↑↓ BOOK FOR CLASS.   'I have to read a big stack of books for class.'

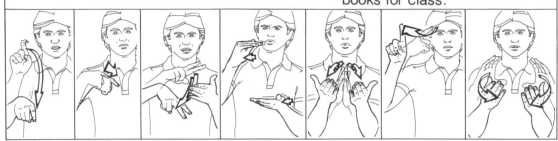

B. STILL LEFT CL:G WINE.   <u>q</u> YOU WANT YOU?   'There's still a little wine left. Do you want some?'

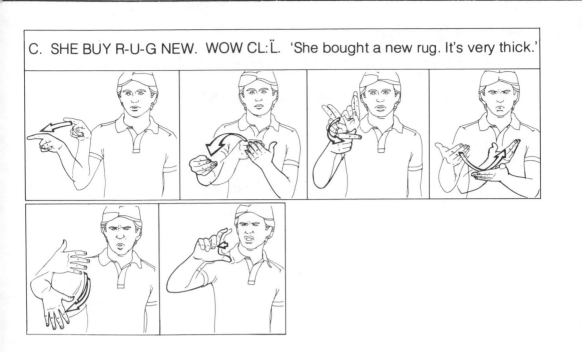

C. SHE BUY R-U-G NEW. WOW CL:L̈. 'She bought a new rug. It's very thick.'

Exercise 13.2:

Substitute the quantifier in the sentence for the one given in parentheses.

EXAMPLE:

CAN SKI, SNOW NOW CL:L̈. 'It's possible to ski; the snow is a few inches deep.'
 (CL:BB↑↓)
  CAN SKI, SNOW NOW CL:BB↑↓. 'It's possible to ski; the snow is very deep.'

<u> t </u>

1. DOG IT WANT CL:G WATER.   (CL:L̈)

2. MY HOUSE WOW DIRTY.   HAVE CL:L̈ D-U-S-T.   (CL:G)

3. BASEMENT, I FIND CL:L̈ WATER.   (CL:BB↑↓)

4. YESTERDAY, CL:L̈ PAPER I THROW-AWAY.   (CL:BB↑↓)

5. CL:G O-J YOU DRINK SHOULD YOU.   (CL:L̈)

6. RECENTLY HE-GIVE-ME CL:L̈ LETTER.   (CL:BB↑↓)

7. RAIN STOP FINISH, LEFT M-U-D CL:G.   (CL:L̈)

More on Plurals

There are two other ways to make plurals of count nouns. (Two ways were discussed earlier in Lesson 7.) They are:

1. Add a classifier which functions as a quantifier, such as CL:5̈, either before the noun or at the end of the sentence.

EXAMPLE:

I SEE CAT CL:5̈5̈.   'I saw a large number of cats.'

I SEE CL:5̈5̈ CAT.   'I saw a large number of cats.'

2. Some nouns can be reduplicated, that is, the sign can be made again several times as it is moved to the side (represented by ++).

EXAMPLE:

IT HOME HAVE TREE ++.   'There are many trees near my home.'

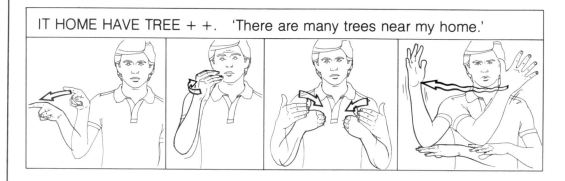

144

Exercise 13.3:

Change the form of the plural nouns in the sentences below to the plural form given in parentheses.

EXAMPLE:

SHE BRING-THERE 5 SUITCASE.   'She brought 5 suitcases there.'
  (Reduplicate)
    SHE BRING-THERE SUITCASE ++.   'She brought many suitcases there.'

1. STORE IT HAVE SEVERAL BICYCLE.   (CL:55̈)

2. H-O-T-E-L IT HAVE MANY DOOR.   (Reduplicate)

3. MY SISTER FINISH HAVE 5 BOYFRIEND.   (CL:55̈)

4. I LIKE HOUSE WITH WINDOW MANY.   (Reduplicate)

5. THERE PARTY I SEE A-FEW CHILDREN.   (CL:55̈)

6. I MUST WRITE 4 LIST.   (Reduplicate)

7. HE HAVE MANY BEAUTIFUL GLASS.   (Reduplicate)

More on Using Numbers

1. The sign for 1-CENT or 'penny' is:

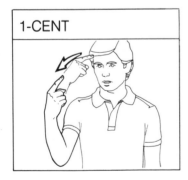

1-CENT

Other numbers can be incorporated in this sign to indicate different amounts:

EXAMPLES:

A. I HAVE 25-CENT I. 'I have a quarter.'

B. WE MUST PAY-HIM 30-CENT. 'We have to pay him 30 cents.'

2. The sign for 1-DOLLAR is:

1-DOLLAR

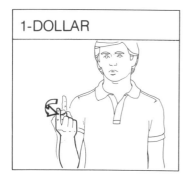

The numbers 1 through 10 can be incorporated in this sign. The numbers 11 and greater do not incorporate; they are followed by a separate sign, DOLLAR.

EXAMPLES:

   _ t _
A. FOOD COST 5-DOLLAR IT. 'The food cost 5 dollars.'

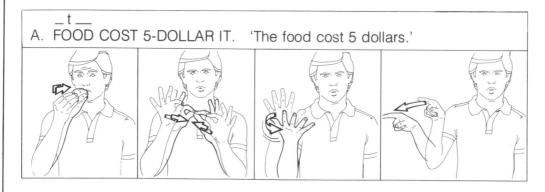

B. 25 DOLLAR YOU OWE-ME. 'You owe me 25 dollars.'

Exercise 13.4:

Substitute the amount given in parentheses for the amount in the sentences below.

EXAMPLE:

$$\overline{\text{q}}$$
YOU HAVE 10-CENT YOU? 'Do you have a dime?'

  (5-CENT)

$$\overline{\text{q}}$$
YOU HAVE 5-CENT YOU? 'Do you have a nickel?'

$$\overline{\text{t}}$$
1. BIRTHDAY HE-GIVE-ME 5-DOLLAR. (7-DOLLAR)

2. I FIND 1-CENT YESTERDAY I. (50-CENT)

3. I WIN 500 DOLLAR I. (300 DOLLAR)

4. LONG-AGO T-T-Y COST 60 DOLLAR. (40 DOLLAR)

5. LONG-AGO I BUY PENCIL COST 2-CENT. (4-CENT)

$$\overline{\text{t}}$$
6. MY CAR OLD SELL 150 DOLLAR. (450 DOLLAR)

$$\overline{\text{q}}$$
7. 10-DOLLAR YOU NEED TODAY? (20 DOLLAR)

Vocabulary

A-LITTLE

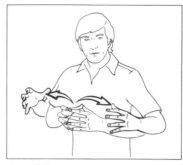

A-LOT, much

ALWAYS

APPOINTMENT, RESERVE, reservation

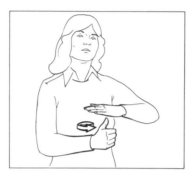

BASEMENT, below, beneath

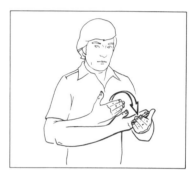

BORN, BIRTHDAY, birth

BOYFRIEND

1-CENT, penny

CHEESE

COST, value, worth, price

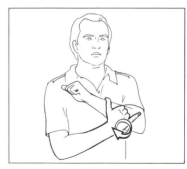

COUNTRY

148

CRAZY-FOR, favorite

DISCUSS, debate, argue

1-DOLLAR

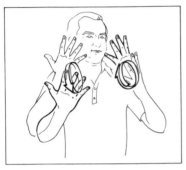

EMBARRASS

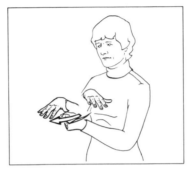

ENOUGH

FREE, safe

FUN

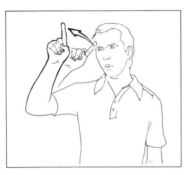

INTELLIGENT, smart

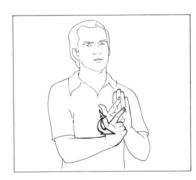

LAW, legal

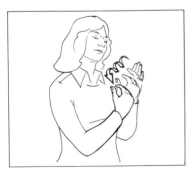

LIST, outline

NATIONAL, nation

OFTEN, frequently

149

OWE, debt, obligation

PIE

PLENTY

PRICE, cost, charge, tax

REASON, realize, rationale

RIGHT (legal, moral)

RULE

SKI
Noun: SKIING

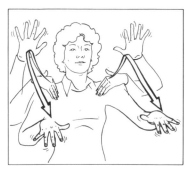

SNOW

SOME

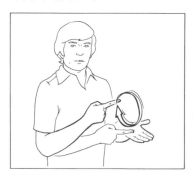

SOMETIMES, occasionally

STRANGE, odd, peculiar, weird

THROW-AWAY, discard

TROUBLE

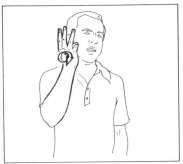 

WINE

WITH, together

151

NOTES

DIALOGUE 4

Bill makes arrangements with Jack to see a new play with Deaf actors. Social and cultural events such as plays, festivals, workshops, and banquets make up a regular part of life in local deaf communities. Sometimes these events are organized and performed by Deaf people and sometimes they are public events made available to Deaf people by sign language interpreters. After such events, as illustrated in the following dialogue, it is common for Deaf people to get together elsewhere to prolong the opportunity to socialize with each other.

            ————————— q —————————————
Bill: KNOW-THAT HAVE PERFORMANCE NEW? DEAF PERFORMANCE

                                     ————— q—————
          GROUP THERE L-A ESTABLISH.   WANT SEE YOU?

          — y —   ————— q—————
Jack: I WANT.   CHAIR LEFT HAVE?

Bill: SHOULD HAVE LEFT CL:5̈.   I-TTY-IT, TWO-US RESERVE
          CHAIR.
          — t —
          TICKET COST 3-DOLLAR.
                               ————————— q —————————————
Jack: I-PAY-YOU NOW CAN I.   WANT TWO-US WITH DRIVE-THERE?

Bill: FINE.   TWO-US WATCH PERFORMANCE FINISH, GO-THERE
          FRIEND HOUSE PARTY, CHAT FRIEND FINISH, COME-HERE
          HOME.
                          — whq —
Jack: TOMORROW I-MEET-YOU TIME?

Bill: TIME 4.   TWO-US TIME PLENTY DRIVE-THERE.

LESSON 14

More Negatives

There are other ways to form negative sentences:

1. Use of NEVER. NEVER occurs either before the verb or at the end of the sentence.
   EXAMPLE:

```
_____ n _____
I EXERCISE NEVER I.    'I never exercise.'
```

```
_____ n _____
I NEVER EXERCISE I.    'I never exercise.'
```

2. Use of NONE to mean 'not,' or 'not at all.' Verbs like HAVE, SEE, UNDERSTAND, FEEL, HEAR, EAT, and GET are frequently negated with NONE. NONE may occur either before or after the verb, but when it occurs after the verb, the two signs are often blended together in a single, smooth movement.

   EXAMPLES:

```
_t___ _____ n _____
A.  FRIEND I SEE~ NONE SINCE.    'I haven't seen my friend for a long time.'
```

B. EXPLANATION I UNDERSTAND~NONE I.
'I didn't understand the explanation.' or 'I didn't understand the explanation at all.'
_t_ _____ n _____
C. T-T-Y I HAVE~ NONE I.   'I don't have a TTY.'

Exercise 14.1:

Change the following sentences to negative sentences with the negative sign given.

EXAMPLE:

I GO-AWAY MOVIE I.   'I go to the movies.'
  (NEVER)
  _____ n _____
  I NEVER GO-AWAY MOVIE I.   'I never go to the movies.'
  _____ n _____
  I GO-AWAY MOVIE NEVER I.   'I never go to the movies.'

1. I HEAR YOU MARRY YOU.   (NONE)

  _____ t _____
2. NURSE GIVE-SHOT, I FEEL I.   (NONE)

  _ t _
3. WRENCH STORE IT HAVE.   (NONE)

4. IT C-O HAVE DEAF WORK.   (NONE)

5. MAN INTERACT DEAF HE.   (NEVER)

  _t_
6. C-F HE GET HE.   (NONE)

  _ t _
7. TURKEY I EAT FINISH.   (NONE)

  _____ t _____
8. MONEY YOU-GIVE-HER, I SEE I.   (NONE)

9. SHE-HELP-ME SHE.   (NEVER)

  _t_
10. T-V I UNDERSTAND CAN I.   (NONE)

11. HE BATHE FINISH HE.   (NEVER)

155

Negative Quantifiers

1. NONE may also be used before a noun to show a zero quantity of the noun.

EXAMPLES:

A. I SEE NONE PEOPLE I.   'I saw no people.'

B. I BUY NONE CLOTHES I.   'I bought no clothes.'

2. NOTHING is also used to indicate zero quantity; it is used after the verb

EXAMPLES:

A. I BUY NOTHING I.   'I bought nothing.'

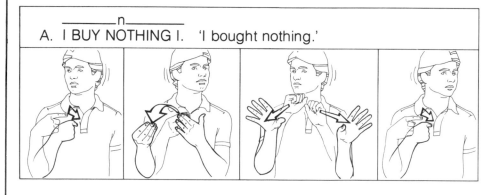

B. I SEE NOTHING I.   'I saw nothing.'

C. HE FEEL NOTHING HE.   'He felt nothing.'

Exercise 14.2:

Change the following sentences to sentences with the negative quantifiers NONE or NOTHING.

EXAMPLE:

<u>   t   </u>
THERE STORE, I SEE A-FEW PEOPLE. 'I saw a few people at the store.'
  (NONE)
      <u>   t   </u> <u>   n   </u>
      THERE STORE, I SEE NONE PEOPLE. 'I saw no people at the store.'

1. SHE BUY HAMMER AND SCREWDRIVER. (NOTHING)

2. NOW YEAR, I GROW V-E-G. (NOTHING)

        <u>   t   </u>
3. NURSE GIVE-SHOT, I FEEL I. (NOTHING)

4. PEOPLE RIDE B-U-S A-FEW. (NONE)

  <u> t </u>
5. Z-O-O IT HAVE MONKEY A-FEW. (NONE)

6. I MUST SHOP, HAVE A-LITTLE FOOD LEFT. (NONE)

     <u>   t </u>
7. WORK P-O, HE EARN A-LOT. (NOTHING)

          <u>   y   </u>
8. REALLY I-INFORM-YOU, HAVE TIME I. (NONE)

9. YESTERDAY FRIEND HE LEARN SIGN. (NONE)

   <u> t </u>
10. A-A-A-D, I DO-WORK. (NOTHING)

Use of NOTHING

In sentences like the following, NOTHING has the meaning of a denial of a preceding accusation. The accusation usually has a topic marker.

EXAMPLES:

       __t_____   _____n_____
A. I HIT BOY, NOTHING I! 'I didn't hit the boy!'

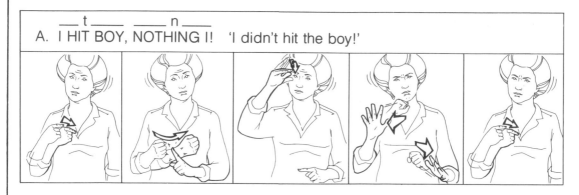

                    _____q_____
B. **Question:** GLASS SHE BREAK? 'Did she break the glass?'
                  _____n_____
   Response: NOTHING SHE. 'No, she didn't.'

Exercise 14.3:

Add NOTHING to the following sentences:

EXAMPLE:

I LOSE YOUR KEY. 'I lost your keys.'
      _____t_____ ____n____
I LOSE YOUR KEY, NOTHING I! 'I didn't lose your keys!'

 _t___
1. LETTER SHE-SEND-HIM.

2. SHIRT NEW WASH-IN-MACHINE.

3. I RESPONSIBLE CAR-ACCIDENT I.

4. I I-TTY-YOU YESTERDAY NIGHT.

5. I I-WARN-HIM FINISH.

6. I-BOTHER-HIM I.

7. BOY STEAL CAMERA HE.

Vocabulary

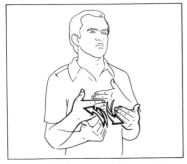

ANYWAY, regardless, it doesn't matter

BATHE
Noun: bath

BOTHER, disturb

CAR-ACCIDENT, collide, collision

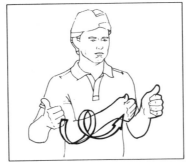

CHASE

CONFUSED, mixed up

CURIOUS

DO-WORK, labor

EARN

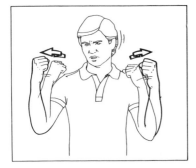

EXERCISE, work out

FALSE, fake

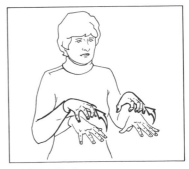

FREEZE, frozen

GIVE-SHOT

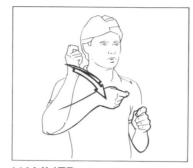

HAMMER

HIT

INTERACT, associate, socialize

LAZY

MONKEY

NERVOUS

NEVER

NONE

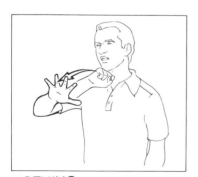

NOTHING

NURSE

PATIENT, patience, endure, bear

160

PLAY

PUZZLED, perplexed

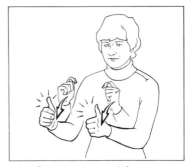

QUICK, fast, rapid

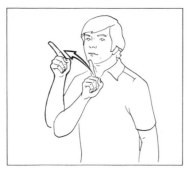

REAL, true

REALLY, TRUE, sure

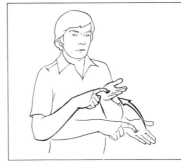

REQUIRE, demand

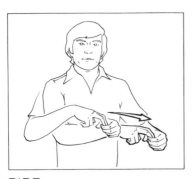

RIDE
Noun: ride,
transportation

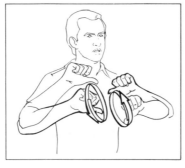

SCIENCE

SCREWDRIVER

SHAVE
Noun: shaver, razor

SHOP, shopping

SHOWER

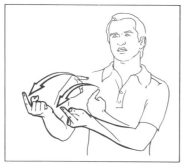

SINCE, lately

SPEND, pay

TAKE-PICTURE
Noun: camera

TURKEY

WARN, caution

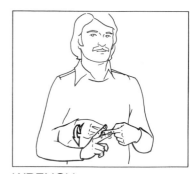

WRENCH

NOTES

LESSON 15

More Directional Verbs

Some directional verbs such as CHOOSE, COPY, TAKE, SUMMON, TAKE-ADVANTAGE-OF and BORROW have a movement opposite of other directional verbs such as GIVE, TELL, SHOW, ASK, INFORM.

I-CHOOSE-YOU	I-GIVE-YOU

I-SUMMON-YOU	I-INFORM-YOU

The other forms of CHOOSE and similar directional verbs are:

YOU-CHOOSE-ME	SHE-CHOOSE-ME

SHE-CHOOSE-HIM	I-CHOOSE-HER
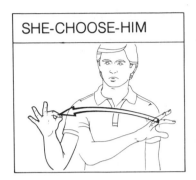	

SHE-CHOOSE-YOU	YOU-CHOOSE-HER
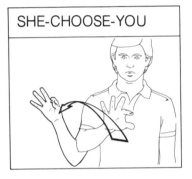	

Exercise 15.1:

Change the following I to you verb forms to I to he/she/it verb forms.

EXAMPLE:

<pre>
                  q
YOUR PAPER I-COPY-YOU CAN I?   'Can I copy from your paper?'
                  q
HER PAPER I-COPY-HER CAN I?   'Can I copy from her paper?'
</pre>

<pre>
                          q
1. DON'T-MIND I-BORROW-YOU DICTIONARY?
                              n
2. I UNDERSTAND.   I DON'T-WANT I-TAKE-ADVANTAGE-YOU.
   __ t __
3. READY, I HAPPY I-SUMMON-YOU.
            t
4. YOUR SCHEDULE I-COPY-YOU CAN I.

5. I WANT I-CHOOSE-YOU.
</pre>

165

Exercise 15.2:

Change the following <u>you to me</u> verb forms to <u>you to he/she/it</u> verb forms.

    EXAMPLE:

    YOU-TELL-ME FINISH YOU-CHOOSE-ME FOR COMMITTEE.
    'You already told me that you picked me for the committee.'
      YOU-TELL-ME FINISH YOU-CHOOSE-HIM FOR COMMITTEE.
      'You already told me that you picked him for the committee.'

        _____ t _____
1. MY HOMEWORK YOU-COPY-ME.
        _____ q _____
2. CAN YOU-TAKE-ME THERE Z-O-O?
        _____ t _____
3. YOU READY LEAVE, YOU-SUMMON-ME.
        _____n_____
4. NOT LIKE YOU-TAKE-ADVANTAGE-ME.

5. SURPRISE YOU-CHOOSE-ME PRESIDENT C-L-U-B.

Directional Verbs Incorporating Two Objects

Directional verbs can change their movement to show the number of persons or objects. The inflection for two objects, YOU-TWO or TWO-THEM has the following form:

I-INFORM-YOU-TWO	I-INFORM-TWO-THEM
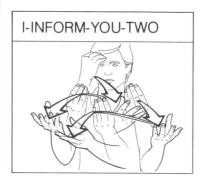	

Exercise 15.3:

Change the following singular object verb forms to dual (two) objects.

EXAMPLE:

HAPPY I I-INFORM-YOU HAPPEN.   'I can let you know what happened.'
　　HAPPY I I-INFORM-YOU-TWO HAPPEN.   'I can let the two of you know what
　　　　　　　　　　　　　　　　　　　　　　happened.'

1. YESTERDAY I I-TELL-HIM, RAIN WILL.

　　— t —
2. MONEY HE-GIVE-HER.

3. BETTER YOU-ASK-HIM. SURE YOU RIGHT YOU.

4. I WANT I-TAKE-YOU THERE RESTAURANT.

5. YOU BEST, I WANT I-CHOOSE-YOU.

6. BEER I-CL:C-GIVE-HER.

　　— t —
7. DAUGHTER I I-SEND-HER LETTER WILL I.

Directional Verbs Incorporating EACH or ALL

Directional verbs also change to indicate 'to each of you/them,' or 'to all of you/them.'
The forms of these inflections are:

I-TELL-EACH-OF-YOU	I-TELL-EACH-OF-THEM

| I-TELL-ALL-OF-YOU | I-TELL-ALL-OF-THEM |

Exercise 15.4:

Change the following singular object verb forms to plural forms using either EACH or ALL as indicated.

EXAMPLE:
 — t ___
TROPHY HE-PRESENT-HER. 'He gave her a trophy.'
 (EACH)
  — t ___
  TROPHY HE-PRESENT-EACH-OF-THEM. 'He gave a trophy to each of them.'

 — t —
1. THIEF COP FINISH HE-CATCH-HER. (EACH)

     ——————— q ———————
2. PLEASE FOR ME, CAN YOU YOU-ASK-HIM? (ALL)

3. WANT I I-INVITE-HER MY WEDDING. (EACH)

4. TOMORROW I I-INFORM-YOU WHO WIN. (ALL)

  _____ t _____
5. MY OLD CLOTHES WILL I I-GIVE-TWO-THEM. (ALL)

6. FINISH I I-TELL-YOU MUST YOU COME-HERE TIME 8. (ALL)

  _____ t _____
7. TWO-OF-THEM CHILDREN MOTHER SHE-SEND-TWO-THEM BOX. (EACH)

Vocabulary

ALONE

BEER

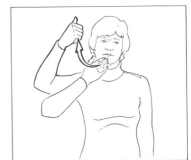

BEST

BETTER

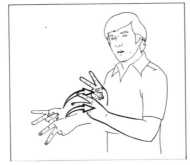

BORROW

CAREFUL, be careful

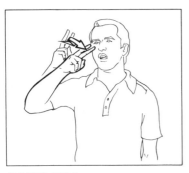

CARELESS

CHOOSE, pick

COMMITTEE

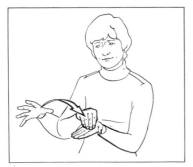

COPY, imitate

DICTIONARY

DON'T-MIND, don't care

DRY, boring

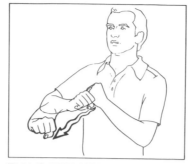

EXAGGERATE

FINALLY, succeed

GOVERNMENT, capitol

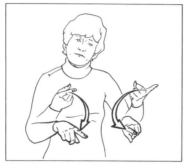

HAPPEN, occur, incident

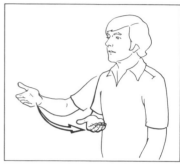

HIRE, INVITE, welcome

IMPOSSIBLE

JEALOUS, envious

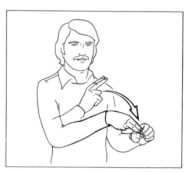

JOIN, participate

KILL, murder

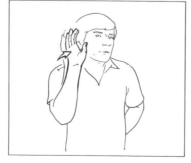

LISTEN

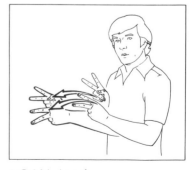

LOAN, lend

MEMBER

OFFER, propose, suggest

POLITE, manners

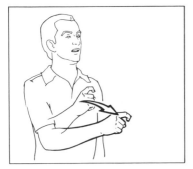

PRESENT, give

READY

SAME-TIME,
simultaneously

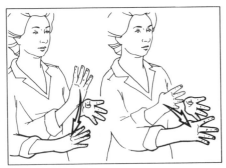

SCHEDULE

SUCCEED, success

SUMMON, call

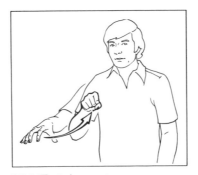

TAKE, take out

TAKE-ADVANTAGE-OF,
rip off

171

THIEF

THIN

TROPHY

WORSE

NOTES

Time Measurements Incorporating Number

The time signs MINUTE, HOUR, DAY, WEEK, and MONTH (but not YEAR) incorporate the numbers 1-9:

5-HOUR

3-DAY

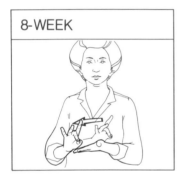

8-WEEK

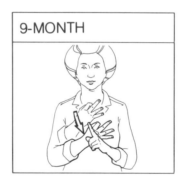

9-MONTH

MINUTE can incorporate the numbers 1-10:

2-MINUTE

but,

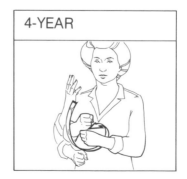

4-YEAR

Exercise 16.1:

Substitute the amount given in parentheses for the amount in the sentences below.

EXAMPLE:

I I-MEET-YOU 2-MINUTE I.   'I'll meet you in 2 minutes.'
   (5-MINUTE)
      I I-MEET-YOU 5-MINUTE I.   'I'll meet you in 5 minutes.'

1. MOVIE IT CONTINUE 2-HOUR.   (3-HOUR)

 __ t __
2. COURSE I TAKE-UP 6-WEEK.   (8-WEEK)

3. NOW TWO-US MARRY 4 YEAR.   (7 YEAR)

4. FIVE-US PLAN GO-AWAY BACKPACKING MAYBE 4-DAY.   (5-DAY)

5. NOW LEFT 3-MONTH, MOVE-AWAY WILL I.   (6-MONTH)

6. I ORDER BED NEW, I MUST WAIT 8-WEEK.   (4-WEEK)

7. HE LOSE ALMOST 8-DAY.   (9-DAY)

Tense Indicators Incorporating Number

The tense indicators NEXT-WEEK, LAST-WEEK, NEXT-MONTH, NEXT-YEAR, and LAST-YEAR can also incorporate some numbers. But they vary in which numbers they can incorporate.

NEXT-WEEK incorporates the numbers 1-9.

LAST-WEEK incorporates the numbers 1-9.

IN-FOUR-WEEK

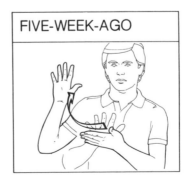

FIVE-WEEK-AGO

NEXT-MONTH incorporates
the numbers 1-9.

NEXT-YEAR incorporates
the numbers 1-5.

IN-SIX-MONTH

IN-THREE-YEAR

LAST-YEAR incorporates
the numbers 1-5.

TWO-YEAR-AGO

Exercise 16.2:

Substitute the tense indicator given in parentheses for the tense indicator in the sentences.

EXAMPLE:

————————— q ——————————
NEXT-WEEK SISTER COME-HERE?   'Is your sister coming next week?'
(IN-TWO-WEEK)

————————— q ——————————
IN-TWO-WEEK SISTER COME-HERE?   'Is your sister coming in 2 weeks?'

1. F-R-A-T MEETING WILL HERE IN-TWO-YEAR.   (IN-FOUR-YEAR)

—— q ——
2. LAST TIME I I-SEE-YOU 3-YEAR-AGO, RIGHT?   (LAST-YEAR)

176

3. 20 YEAR PAST HARD FIND INTERPRETER.   (25 YEAR)

4. PARTY THERE MY HOME IN-TWO-MONTH.   (IN-THREE-MONTH)

5. I GO-THERE FINISH FOUR-WEEK-AGO.   (SIX-WEEK-AGO)

6. HE GRADUATE GALLAUDET 5-YEAR-AGO.   (FOUR-YEAR-AGO)

7. C-O SAY WILL BRING-HERE BED IN-SIX-WEEK.   (IN-FOUR-WEEK)

Time Reduplication

The signs HOUR, WEEK, MONTH, and NEXT-YEAR can be reduplicated to mean 'hourly,' 'weekly,' 'monthly,' and 'yearly.'

EXAMPLE:

I MUST GO-THERE DOCTOR WEEKLY.   'I must go to the doctor every week.'

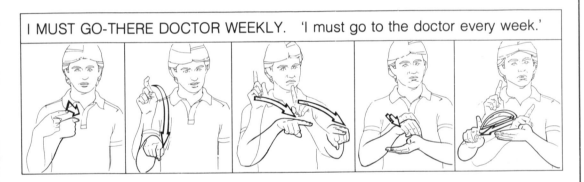

| HOURLY | WEEKLY | MONTHLY |

However, 'daily' has the following form:

YEARLY	DAILY
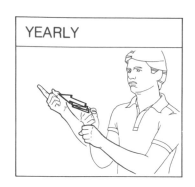	

Exercise 16.3:

Substitute the reduplicated signs in parentheses for those given in the sentences.

EXAMPLE:

__ t ___
FRIEND I SHOULD GO-THERE VISIT DAILY. 'I should go to visit my friend every
day.'

(WEEKLY)
___t__
FRIEND I SHOULD GO-THERE VISIT WEEKLY. 'I should go to visit my friend
every week.'

1. IT-SEND-ME NEWSPAPER WEEKLY.   (MONTHLY)

2. MUST I TAKE-PILL HOURLY.   (DAILY)

3. SHE GO-THERE EUROPE BUSINESS YEARLY.   (MONTHLY)

4. SHE EXERCISE DAILY.   (WEEKLY)

5. HE TO-TELEPHONE I WEEKLY, I BORED I.   (DAILY)

NOTE: More on Time Repetition

Some forms of time that occur regularly are not repeated but use a single movement.
1. To show EVERY-MONDAY, -TUESDAY, -WEDNESDAY, etc., a downward movement is used:

EVERY-SUNDAY	EVERY-SATURDAY

2. To show EVERY-MORNING, -AFTERNOON, -NOON, -NIGHT, a sideward movement is used:

EVERY-MORNING	EVERY-NOON

Vocabulary

ANIMAL

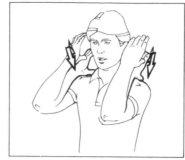

BACKPACKING

BIRD, chicken

BORED

BOSS

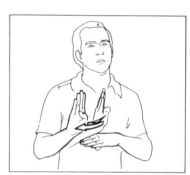

BUSY, business

CITY, town, community

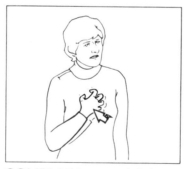

COMPLAIN, complaint, gripe

CONTINUE, last

COW

DAILY, usual, ordinary

DIFFICULT, difficulty

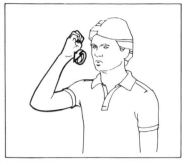 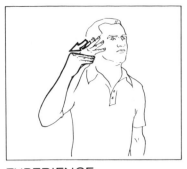 

EUROPE   EXPERIENCE   FISH

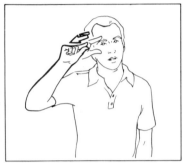 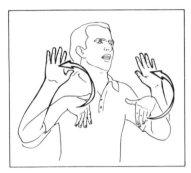 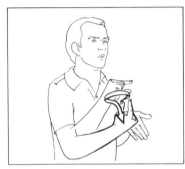

GALLAUDET   GIVE-UP, surrender   GRADUATE

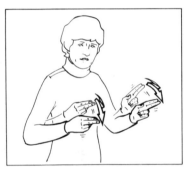 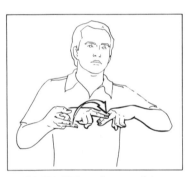 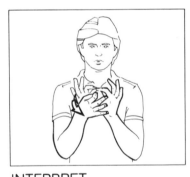

HURRY, rush   INCREASE, raise, add   INTERPRET

INTERRUPT   LAST, final, end   MOUSE

181

MOVE-AWAY

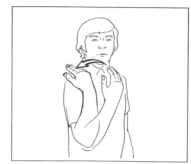

PAST

PIG, pork

PITY, sympathy

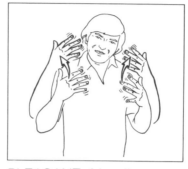

PLEASANT, friendly

PRINT, publish
Noun: NEWSPAPER

SOPHISTICATED, prim

START, begin

TAKE-PILL
Noun: pill

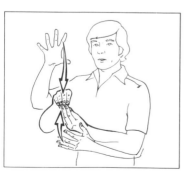

TOTAL, add, add up

DIALOGUE 5

A group of Deaf people are meeting at Bill's home to watch a captioned film. This is a fading tradition. Prior to the development of decoders for video closed captioning, there were captioned films. These were 16mm films collected and subtitled by a government agency and loaned free of charge to groups of Deaf people by mail. Often the films were an excuse to gather and were shown after an evening of dining, playing games, or even business meetings of a club. Today, films are still available for loan but with the advent of video rentals and home VCRs, they are not as much in demand as they once were.

This dialogue also illustrates different types of work situations Deaf people experience. Sometimes they are the only Deaf person at their place of work. Ron is describing how he is attempting to help meet his communication needs by teaching sign to people at his workplace and by getting a teletypewriter (TTY), a device that permits deaf people to type messages to other TTYs via telephone.

              _____ n _____   _ q _

Jane: YOU, I SEE ~NONE SINCE. I HEAR YOU NEW WORK. FINE?

                            _____ t _____ ___ n ___

Ron: FINE. ALONE DEAF. THEY KNOW SIGN NOTHING. I DECIDE
ESTABLISH SIGN CLASS. 2-HOUR EVERY-TUESDAY.

                               _____ q _____

Jane: GOOD IDEA YOU. YOUR BOSS SIGN, FINGERSPELL?

Ron: A-LITTLE. I HAVE 3 BOSS. I PRESENT-EACH SIGN
BOOK. THEY LEARN A-LITTLE. NEXT-WEEK I GET T-T-Y
SHOULD. YOU-TTY-ME CAN YOU.

Jane: WOW FINE. NOW HAVE TOTAL 6 DEAF WORK MY C-O.

                 _____ q _____
YOUR C-O HIRE DEAF MORE WILL?

                 — y —

Ron: SHOULD.

                 — q —

Bill: READY? NOW MOVIE START.

LESSON 17

Using a Clause as Topic

1. Some verbs such as WANT, DON'T-WANT, KNOW, DON'T-KNOW, LIKE, DON'T-LIKE, KNOW-THAT, FEEL, DECIDE, HOPE, SEE, DOUBT, TEND can be preceded by a topicalized clause.

EXAMPLES:

```
            _____ t _____   _____ n _____
   A.  GO-AWAY TOMORROW, I DON'T-WANT I.   'I don't want to leave tomorrow.'
```

```
         _____ t _____   _____ y _____
   B.  HE LIKE SHE GIRL, I KNOW-THAT I.   'I know that he likes the girl.'
         _____ t _____   ____ n _____
   C.  TWO-US LEAVE TIME 7 MORNING, SHE DOUBT.   'She doubts that we will
       leave at 7 A.M.'
```

2. Also, the negatives NOT, NEVER, NONE and NOTHING can be preceded by a topicalized clause.

EXAMPLES:

```
         _____ t _____   __ n _
   A.  GO-AWAY TOMORROW, NOT I.   'I'm not leaving tomorrow.'
         ____ t ____  __ n __
   B.  I EXERCISE, NEVER.   'I never exercise.'
```

Exercise 17.1:

Change the following sentences to sentences with topicalized clauses.

EXAMPLE:

<u>   y   </u>
I KNOW-THAT HE AGAIN LATE.   'I know he'll be late again.'
<u>   t   y   </u>
HE AGAIN LATE, I KNOW-THAT.   'I know he'll be late again.'

<u>   n   </u>
1. I DON'T-KNOW FINISH ADVERTISE TOURNAMENT.

<u>   n   </u>
2. HE DOUBT HE APPLY FOR PRESIDENT.

3. TWO-THEM TEND ARGUE ALL-DAY.

4. HE KNOW-THAT I SUPPORT WHEELCHAIR.

<u>   n   </u>
5. SHE DON'T-WANT BORROW MONEY FROM BOSS.

<u>   n   </u>
6. I DON'T-WANT I AGAIN BROKE.

7. THREE-US WANT GO-BY-BOAT THERE EUROPE.

<u>   n   </u>
8. HE NOT FIRED.

9. GRANDFATHER LIKE TELL-STORY.

<u>   n   </u>
10. I DON'T-LIKE STAY PARTY ALL-NIGHT.

Comparative Sentences

When comparing two persons, places, things or ideas, the following procedure is used.
1. First establish one person, place, thing or idea on one side of the body and the other on the other side.
2. Then indicate which one you will comment upon.

EXAMPLES:

_____ t _____
A. WASHINGTON, NEW-YORK, I PREFER IT. (Washington).
'I prefer Washington to New York.'

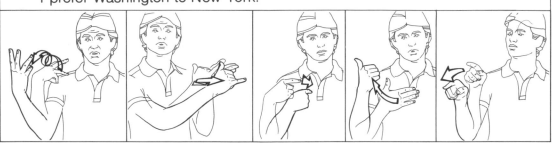

_____ t _____
B. CAR IT HAVE RADIO, A-C; IT PLAIN, I WANT IT. (the plain one).
'I want the plain car rather than the one with a radio and air conditioner.'

3. A person, place, thing or idea can be established in a pronoun location to show a relationship with that pronoun.

_____ t _____
C. MY SISTER, YOUR SISTER, SHE (my sister) OLDER SHE.
'My sister is older than yours.'

Exercise 17.2:

Combine the following sentences to form comparative sentences.

EXAMPLE:

HE COOK HE.   HE WASH-DISH HE.   'He cooks. He washes dishes.'
  (PREFER)
  _____ t _____
  COOK, WASH-DISH, HE PREFER IT.   'He prefers to cook rather than to wash
                                                            dishes.'

1. HOUSE R-E-N-T, A-P-T R-E-N-T.   (WORSE)

2. IT WOOD TABLE, IT METAL TABLE.   (WANT)

3. STAY HOME WATCH T-V, GO-AWAY MOVIE PAY 5-DOLLAR.   (BETTER)

4. IT FLOWER REAL, IT FLOWER S-I-L-K.   (PRETTIER)

   _____ q _____
5. IT EXPENSIVE, IT CHEAP.   (YOU WANT?)

6. I GO-THERE COLLEGE, I STAY WORK.   (STAY)

7. MEETING HERE, MEETING THERE.   (PREFER)

Conjunctions

The signs WRONG, HAPPEN, HIT, FRUSTRATE, and FIND can be used as conjunctions. Some of their meanings as conjunctions are:

WRONG   'without warning, suddenly'
FRUSTRATE   'to be prevented from'
HIT   'unexpectedly, turned out that'
FIND   'find out that'
HAPPEN   'happened that'

EXAMPLES:

A. I WALK, WRONG RAIN.   'As I was walking, it suddenly started raining.'

——————— n ——————

B. I PLAN PARTY, FIND HE CAN'T COME-HERE.
   'I was planning the party, then I found out that he couldn't come.'
C. HE GO-AWAY VACATION 1-WEEK, HIT LAID-UP SICK.
   'He went on vacation for a week and unexpectedly became ill.'
D. I CHAT HAPPEN HE-TELL-ME HE FROM WASHINGTON.
   'I was talking with him and he happened to tell me he was from Washington.'
E. TONIGHT TWO-US WANT SEE MOVIE, FRUSTRATE CLOSE.
   'We wanted to see the movie tonight but it was closed.'

Exercise 17.3:

Combine the sentences below, using the conjunction given.

EXAMPLE:

TWO-THEM STEADY-DATE 6-MONTH.   'They were dating for 6 months'.
TWO-THEM MARRY.   'They got married.'
   (WRONG)
      TWO-THEM STEADY-DATE 6-MONTH, WRONG MARRY.
      'They were dating for 6 months, and before you knew it they got married.'

1. SHE RESEARCH A-S-L.
   SHE FIND RULE + +.   (HIT)

2. SHE GO-THERE BUY T-T-Y.
   T-T-Y S-A-L-E.   (HAPPEN)

3. BABY SEEM SICK.
   BABY HAVE EAR-ACHE.   (FIND)

4. CLOTHES PUT-IN WASH-IN-MACHINE.
   CLOTHES RUIN.   (FRUSTRATE)

5. I BUY GLASS NEW.
   GLASS DAMAGE.   (WRONG)

6. TWO-US CHAT.
   TWO-US SAME HAVE DEAF PARENTS.   (FIND)

7. I WATCH T-V.
   T-V CAPTION.   (WRONG)

8. I DRIVE-THERE.
   SHE NOT HOME.   (FRUSTRATE)

9. HE HAVE NEW CAR.
   CAR STEAL.   (FRUSTRATE)

10. HE ACT NOTHING-TO-IT.
    HE SHOT-UP FAMOUS.   (WRONG)

Vocabulary

APPLY, volunteer,
candidate

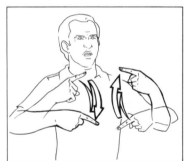

ARGUE, quarrel

BROKE

BUT

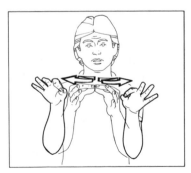

CAPTION, sub-titles

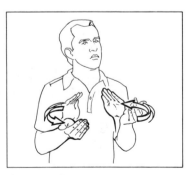

COMPARE
Noun: comparison

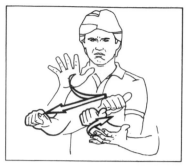

DAMAGE, destroy

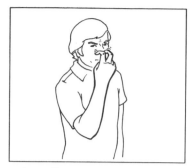

DOUBT

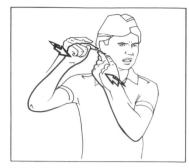

EARACHE

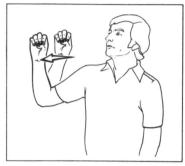

EAST

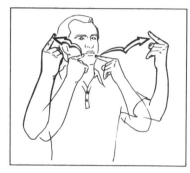

FAMOUS

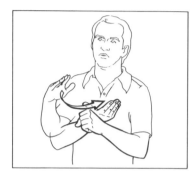

FIRE (from job)

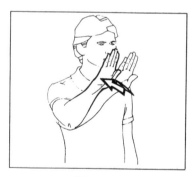

FRUSTRATE

FRUSTRATE (conjunction)

HIT (conjunction)

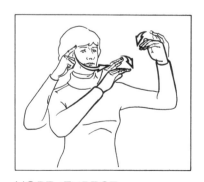

HOPE, EXPECT

LAID-UP

LATE

LIE-DOWN

METAL

NAB, get ahold of

NORTH

NOTHING-TO-IT

PUT-IN

RADIO

RENT

RESEARCH

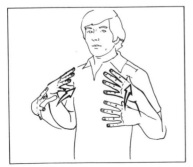

RETIRE, loaf
Noun: VACATION

RUBBER

RUIN, spoiled

 SEEM, appears

 SHOT-UP, become successful

 SOMETHING, someone, alone

 SOUTH

 STEADY-DATE

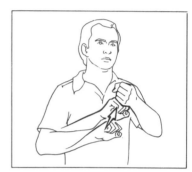 SUPPORT, sponsor, advocate

 TEND

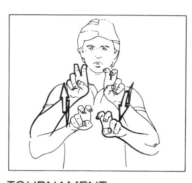 TOURNAMENT

 WEST

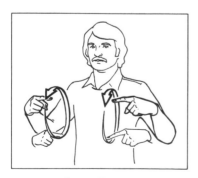 WHEELCHAIR

 WOOD

 WRONG (conjunction)

NOTES

LESSON 18

Verb Inflection: -REPEATEDLY

Many action verbs can be repeated to show a repeated or regular action. Frequently the following facial adverbs are used with verbs inflected for -REPEATEDLY.

'with effort or difficulty'

'with ease, pleasure'	'with attention, care, deliberately'	'without attention, carelessly, foolishly'

EXAMPLE:

```
        ____t____
```
A. DEAF GROUP I LIKE GO-THERE-REPEATEDLY CHAT.
    'I like to go often to talk with deaf people.'

$$\overline{\qquad\qquad \text{n} \qquad\qquad}$$
B. DAILY I-TELL-HER-REPEATEDLY, SHE NOT UNDERSTAND.
   'I've told her every day, but she still doesn't understand.'
$$\overline{\qquad\qquad \text{n} \qquad}$$
C. SINCE LETTER I I-SEND-HIM-REPEATEDLY, HEAR~NONE I.
   'I kept sending him letters, but I heard nothing from him.'

Exercise 18.1:

Change the following underlined verb forms to the -REPEATEDLY form, and use the facial adverb given in parentheses.

EXAMPLE:

TWO-THEM CHILDREN FIGHT.   'The two children got into a fight.'
   (with effort)
     TWO-THEM CHILDREN FIGHT-REPEATEDLY.   'The two children fight all the
                                             time.'

1. YESTERDAY NIGHT I-TTY-YOU, YOU NONE YOU.   (with effort)

$$\overline{\qquad\qquad \text{t} \qquad\qquad}$$
2. PITY-HIM, TEAM HIS LOUSY, HE LOSE-COMPETITION.   (carelessly)

3. BROTHER TEND ANALYZE MOVIE.   (with attention)

4. SHE BOTHER-HIM, WRONG HE-BAWL-OUT-HER.   (carelessly)

$$\overline{\quad \text{t} \quad}$$
5. HE THIRSTY.   WATER HE DRINK.   (with effort)

6. SHE LOVE READ.   (with ease)

$$\overline{\qquad\quad \text{t} \quad\quad}$$
7. BASKETBALL, NEW-YORK BEFORE WIN.   (with ease)

8. FINISH I-WARN-YOU SHOULD FIX T-I-R-E.   (with effort)

9. BORED I I-PRESENT-YOU MONEY.   (with effort)

10. FIND HE INFORM-HIM POLICE.   (with attention)

Verb Inflection: -CONTINUALLY

Many verbs can show a continuing action by adding a circular movement. Facial adverbs used with -REPEATEDLY can also be used with the -CONTINUALLY inflection.

EXAMPLES:

A. B-U-S NOT COME-HERE, I STAND-CONTINUALLY.
   'I stood around waiting for the bus. It didn't come.'

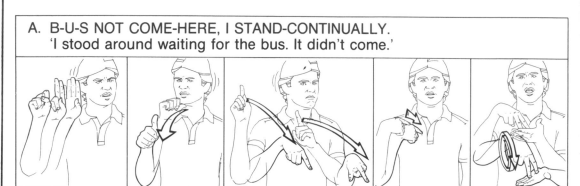

B. ALL-DAY I WORK-CONTINUALLY, NOT EXPECT TIME 6 I.
   'I worked without stopping all day and didn't realize it was 6 o'clock.'

Exercise 18.2:

Change the underlined verb forms to the -CONTINUALLY form, and use the facial adverb given in parentheses.

EXAMPLE:

___ t ___
DENTIST, I WAIT.   'I sat waiting for the dentist.'
   (with effort)
      ___ t ___
      DENTIST, I WAIT-CONTINUALLY.   'I sat for a long while waiting for the dentist.'

1. HE STAY-THERE 3-HOUR FINISH COME-HERE.   (with ease)

2. HE APPEAR NONE, I WAIT.   (with effort)

3. TRAVEL, I WANT.   (with effort)

4. SHE <u>EAT</u>, WRONG BECOME-FAT. (carelessly)

5. HARD UNDERSTAND HE <u>FINGERSPELL</u>. (with attention)

6. WOOD <u>BURN</u> 3-HOUR. (with ease)

7. HOMEWORK I <u>STRUGGLE</u>, FINALLY UNDERSTAND I. (with effort)

Vocabulary

ANALYZE, research

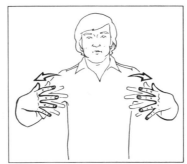

BECOME-FAT

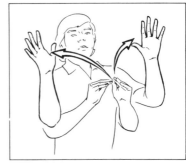

BRIGHT, CLEAR, obvious

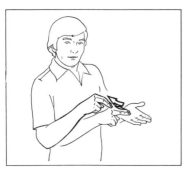

BUTTER

CELEBRATE, anniversary

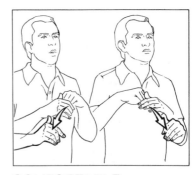

COMFORTABLE

CONFIDENT, confidence

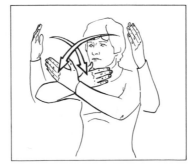

DARK

DENTIST

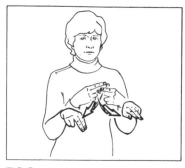

EGG

ELECTRIC, electricity

EMPHASIZE, impress, stress

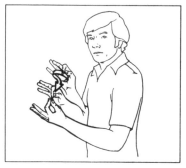

EXACT, perfect, precise

FIGHT

FIX

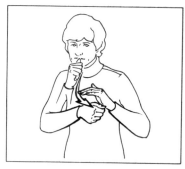

HIDE

IMPRESSED

JUMP

KNEEL

LICENSE

LONG (time)

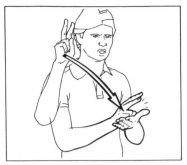

LOSE-COMPETITION

LOUSY

MIRROR

MUSIC, song

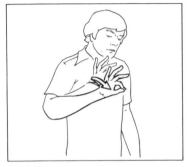

PEPPER

POISON

POTATO

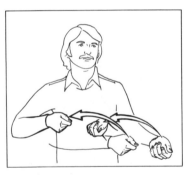

PULL

PUSH

SALT

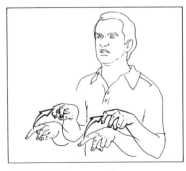

SELFISH, greedy

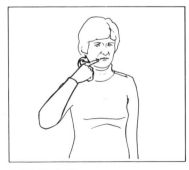

SOUR, bitter

STAND

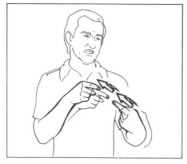

STRUGGLE

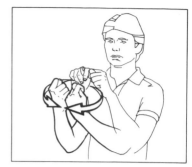

TEAM

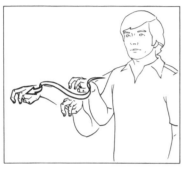

TRAVEL, tour

VERY

NOTES

Adjective Modulation: VERY-

Some adverbs are formed by changing the movement of the adjective. The movement added to adjectives to mean 'very' has the following form:
1. The beginning of the sign has a hold which appears "tense,"
2. Then there is a quick release.
Note the facial adverb commonly used with the VERY-modulation shown below.

MAD	VERY-MAD

FAST	VERY-FAST
	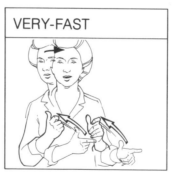

SLOW	VERY-SLOW

Exercise 19.1:

Change the adjectives in the following sentences by adding the modulation VERY-.

EXAMPLE:

BUILDING IT OLD.   'The building is old.'
    BUILDING IT VERY-OLD.   'The building is very old.'

1. K-A-N-S-A-S CL:BB.

2. WINTER THERE M-I-N-N COLD.

3. HER HOME WOW SMALL.

4. SNOW ALL-OVER WOW WHITE.

5. YOUR LECTURE CLEAR.

    _____ n _____
6. YOU WORK NOTHING, LAZY YOU.

7. BASKETBALL PLAYER HE WOW TALL.

8. GAS NOW EXPENSIVE.

9. MUST YOU GO-THERE MEETING, IT IMPORTANT.

    ____ t ____
10. RAIN SINCE, WOW WORSE.

Adjective Modulation: -REPEATEDLY

The movement of some adjectives can be repeated to show the meaning of 'repeatedly.' This movement is added to adjectives which describe a condition which starts, stops, and then starts again.
    Examples of these adjectives are:

ANGRY	MAD	FRUSTRATED	WRONG
SICK	EMBARRASSED	GUILTY	CARELESS
AFRAID	WORRY	NOISE	
HURT	LATE	DIFFERENT	

MAD	MAD-REPEATEDLY

WRONG	WRONG-REPEATEDLY

Exercise 19.2:

Change the underlined adjectives in the following sentences by adding the modulation -REPEATEDLY.

EXAMPLE:

I-TELL-HIM-REPEATEDLY. HE CARELESS.
  'I have told him many times. He's careless.'
  I-TELL-HIM-REPEATEDLY. HE CARELESS-REPEATEDLY.
    I have told him many times. He still gets careless.'

               __ whq _
1. SHE MAD.   WRONG?

2. FOOTBALL PLAYER HE HURT.

3. FATHER WORRY.   I LATE I.

        _____ n _____
4. SINCE DON'T-KNOW WHY, I SICK.

5. DOWNSTAIRS HAVE DOG, NOISE AWFUL.

6. HE JUDGMENT NONE, HE <u>WRONG</u>.

7. HE LOOK-FOR WORK, <u>FRUSTRATE</u> HE.

Adjective Modulation:-CONTINUALLY

Adjectives can also be inflected to show the meaning of 'continually.' This inflection is made by adding a circular movement.
Examples of these adjectives are:

CAREFUL	HURT	SILLY	MAD
WRONG	DIFFERENT	EMBARRASSED	FRUSTRATED
AFRAID	SICK	MISCHIEVOUS	

CAREFUL
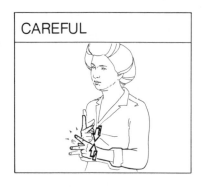

CAREFUL-CONTINUALLY

HURT

HURT-CONTINUALLY

Exercise 19.3:

Change the underlined adjectives in the following sentences by adding the modulation -CONTINUALLY.

EXAMPLE:

AWFUL HE FALL, BREAK L-E-G.   SINCE <u>HURT</u>.
  'It's terrible! He fell and broke his leg. Since then it has hurt.'
AWFUL HE FALL, BREAK L-E-G.   SINCE HURT-CONTINUALLY.
    'It's terrible! He fell and broke his leg. Since then it has hurt all the time.'

1. LIKE I OUTSIDE SIT, LOOK-AT PEOPLE <u>DIFFERENT</u>.

    _____ t _____
2. PARTY THERE, SHE <u>EMBARRASSED</u> ALL-NIGHT.

    _____ n _____
3. I DON'T-KNOW, SEEM I <u>WRONG</u>.

4. HE BUY NEW CAR, SINCE <u>CAREFUL</u> HE.

5. AUNT <u>SICK</u>.   WRONG LOST #JOB.

6. ALL-DAY GIRL <u>MISCHIEVOUS</u>.

    _____ t _____
7. CAPTION T-V HAVE <u>DIFFERENT-REPEATEDLY</u>.

Vocabulary

ACTION, activities

AFRAID

APPREHENSIVE, guilty

BACK

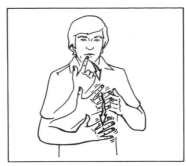

BLOOD

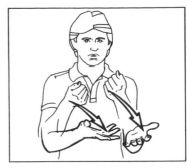

CAUSE

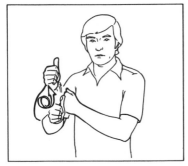

DANGER, dangerous,
threat

DISMISS, lay off, pardon,
excuse

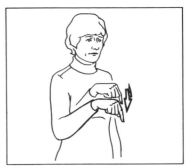

DOWNSTAIRS

EACH, every

EITHER

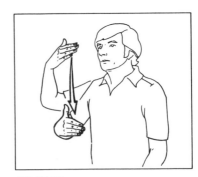

FRONT

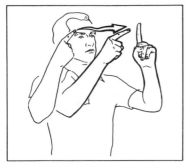

GOAL, aim, objective

GUESS, assume,
estimate

HABIT, custom, used to

207

HISTORY

IMAGINE

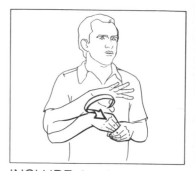

INCLUDE, involve, everything

#JOB

JUDGE, court

LAND

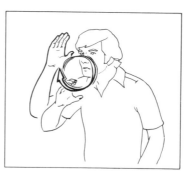

LOOK-FOR, search, hunt

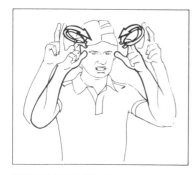

MISCHIEVOUS

OCEAN

OUTDOORS, outside

PRAISE, commend,
applaud

PREVENT, block

PROVE, proof

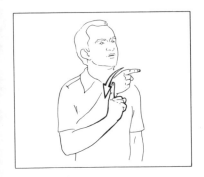

RIVER Cross fingers
into 'r'

ROUGH

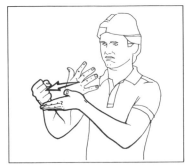

RUN-OUT-OF, deplete

SILLY, ridiculous

SUPPOSE, imagine, if

SUPPRESS, restrain

SWALLOW

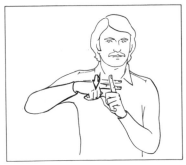

TEMPERATURE

TOUGH

TURN-DOWN, reject   UPSTAIRS   WEIGH, weight, pound

DIALOGUE 6

Don is reminiscing about the "old days" before TTYs and when things were cheaper. Before devices existed to allow Deaf people to communicate via telephone, there was always a risk you might not find your friend at home should you stop in for a visit. Since TTYs were not widely available to Deaf people until the 1970's, many Deaf people today remember this experience. In fact, some still like to drop by a friend's house without calling ahead first.

Don:
_____ t _____ _____ n _____
LONG-AGO NONE HAVE T-T-Y, T-V CAPTION, INTERPRETER

_____
SAME NOW.   YOU-PL. YOUNG HAVE PLENTY.

Mary:
_____ t _____ _____ whq _____
FIRST T-T-Y YOU BUY WHEN?

Don: LONG-AGO 1971.

Mary:
_____ whq _____
HOW-MUCH COST?

Don:
_____ t _____
60 DOLLAR.   T-T-Y LONG-AGO VERY-BIG, NOW VERY-SMALL,

COST 600 DOLLAR.

Mary: WOW.   IMPORTANT HAVE T-T-Y.

Don: TRUE.   I REMEMBER I WANT GO-THERE VISIT FRIEND, MUST I

DRIVE-THERE.   SOMETIMES I DRIVE-THERE, FRUSTRATE

FRIEND NOT THERE.   MUST GO-THERE-REPEATEDLY FINALLY

NAB FRIEND.   MANY TIME I FRUSTRATE-REPEATEDLY.

Mary: NOW I-TTY-HIM FRIEND, FIND HE NOT HOME.   I SAVE GAS.

Don:
_____ t _____
TRUE.   COMPARE LONG-AGO, NOW IT(now) BETTER.

LESSON 20

Conditional Sentences

Conditional sentences have two parts: *the condition* and *the consequence*. The sentences are made by:

1. Raising the eyebrows during the *condition* (represented by _____ if _____), and lowering them during the *consequence*.
2. Optionally the *condition* may be preceded by either SUPPOSE or #IF.

EXAMPLES:

_____ if _____
A. TOMORROW SNOW, I GO-AWAY SKIING.   'If it snows tomorrow, I'll go skiing.'

_____if _____
B. SUPPOSE THERE HAVE INTERPRETER, I GO-THERE I.
'If there is an interpreter, I'll go.'

_____ if _____
C. #IF I HEAR~NONE, I PROCEED WILL I.
'If I don't hear anything, I'll go ahead.'

Exercise 20.1:

Combine the following sentences into conditional sentences, using the first sentence as the "condition" and the second as the "consequence."

EXAMPLE:

BOOK NOT ARRIVE.　'The books haven't arrived.'
I PROCEED CLASS.　'I'll go ahead with my class.'
_____if_____
BOOKS NOT ARRIVE, I PROCEED CLASS.
'If the books haven't arrived, I'll go ahead with my class.'

1. AIRPLANE AGAIN POSTPONE.
   I MAD I.

2. MONEY YOU-GIVE-ME NOW.
   I BUY TICKET I.

    _t _
3. C-F I GET FINISH.
   I-INFORM-ALL-OF-YOU.

4. YOU DRIVE-THERE.
   I GO-WITH WANT I.

5. T-V CAPTION HAVE HE.
   I GO-THERE HIS HOME.

6. T-V HAVE ACTOR DEAF IT.
   I WATCH MUST I.

7. LEARN SIGN HE WANT.
   PRACTICE MUST HE.

Rhetorical Questions

WH-question signs can be used as rhetorical questions to draw attention to additional information which the signer will provide. However, rhetorical questions differ from ordinary WH-questions in that the eyebrows are raised instead of squeezed together. _____rq _____ indicates raised eyebrows for the rhetorical question.

EXAMPLES:

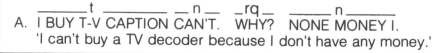

    _____t _____ _n__ _rq_ _____n_____
A. I BUY T-V CAPTION CAN'T. WHY? NONE MONEY I.
    'I can't buy a TV decoder because I don't have any money.'

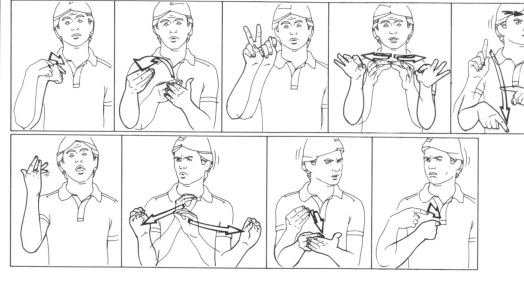

                                              _rq_ _____n_____
B. WILL INFORM-ALL-OF-YOU ABOUT MEETING. WHEN? DON'T-KNOW I.
    'I don't know when I will inform you of the meeting.'
                                   _rq_
C. SISTER GO-THERE COLLEGE. WHERE? GALLAUDET.
    'My sister is going to Gallaudet College.'

Exercise 20.2:

Add the information in the second sentence to the first sentence, using the WH-question sign given.

EXAMPLE:

I GO-AWAY WASHINGTON.   'I'm going to Washington.'
  (HOW)
    I GO-BY-TRAIN   'I'm going by train.'
                       _rq_
    I GO-AWAY WASHINGTON. HOW? GO-BY-TRAIN.
    'I'm going to Washington by train.'

1. THEY FINISH VOTE PRESIDENT C-L-U-B.   (WHO)
   BROTHER PRESIDENT C-L-U-B HE.

2. NOW RESEARCH-REPEATEDLY SIGN.   (WHAT-FOR)
   UNDERSTAND LANGUAGE.

   _t _
3. CAR I FINISH DECIDE BUY.   (WHICH)
   D-A-T-S-U-N I BUY.

4. HE LECTURE-REPEATEDLY.   (WHAT)
   HE LECTURE ABOUT C-L-E-R-C, HIMSELF DEAF.

5. I GO-THERE PUT-IN-GAS.   (HOW-MUCH)
   GAS COST 20 DOLLAR.

6. YOU GO-TO-IT CLOSE-DOOR.   (WHY)
   BUG ENTER-REPEATEDLY.

beer = "b" against cheek

subway: palm ↓ floor "y" across it

Vocabulary

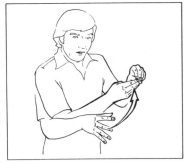

ADD-TO, additional

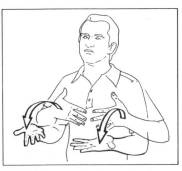

ADMIT, confess

ADULT

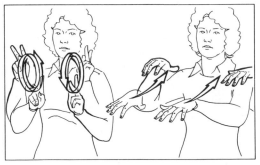

AUDIENCE

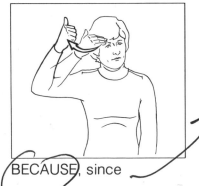

BECAUSE, since

with pointer

215

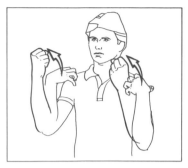 BRAVE

 BUG, insect

 CHANGE, alter, modify

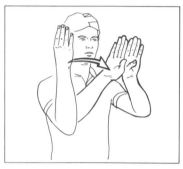 CLOSE-DOOR

 CONTROL, manage, direct

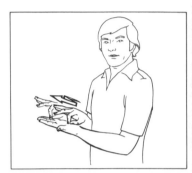 COUNT

 DENY

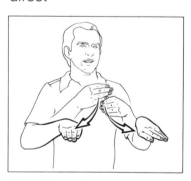 DIVIDE, split

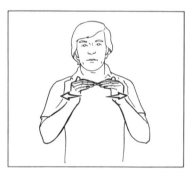 EQUAL, even, fair

 EXCHANGE, switch, trade in

 FOLLOW

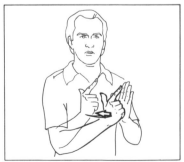 FORBID, illegal, prohibit

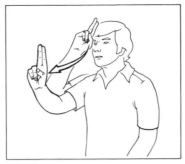

HONEST, truth

HONOR

#IF *or like "judge"*

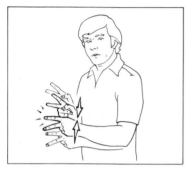

KEEP, be careful

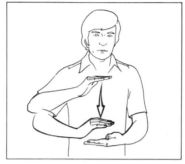

LESS, reduce

LET, allow, permit

LIMIT, restrict

MEAN, cruel

MEASURE

MULTIPLY

OPPOSE, sue, against
Noun: discrimination,
prejudice

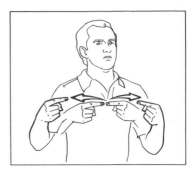

OPPOSITE, counter

POSTPONE, put off

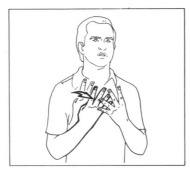

PRISON

PROCEED, get along, go
ahead

PUNISH, penalty

REJECT

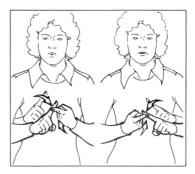

RELATIVES

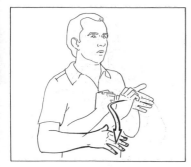
REMOVE, discard

SEPARATE, apart

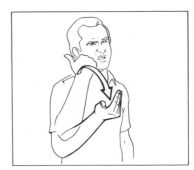
SHAME

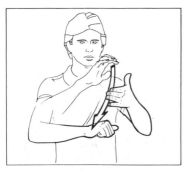
SUBTRACT

VOTE, elect

WASTE

219

Pluralizing Classifiers

Pronominal classifiers can be reduplicated to form plurals. Two ways are shown below.

EXAMPLES:

A. WOW BICYCLE CL:3-IN-A-ROW.	'Wow, there are a lot of bicycles lined up in a row.'

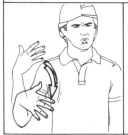  

B. WOW BICYCLE CL:3-ALL-OVER.	'Wow, there are bicycles all over the place.'

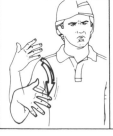  

Some other pronominal classifiers are:

CL:Å

CL: ⊢

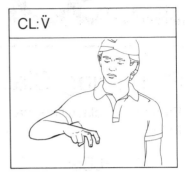

CL:V̈

For any stationary object such as a house, a vase, a statue, a lamp, a company, a business.

For winged aircraft.

For any small or crouched animal or human such as a frog, a mouse, a child sitting down, or a horse lying down.

C. BEFORE NOTHING, NOW HOUSE CL:Å-ALL-OVER.
'Before there was nothing, now there are houses all over the place.'

Exercise 21.1:

Change the plural form in the sentences below to the plural form given in parentheses by using a classifier.

EXAMPLE:

I WALK, SEE RABBIT MANY.   'I was walking and saw many rabbits.'
   (ALL-OVER)
      I WALK, SEE RABBIT CL:V̈-ALL-OVER.   'I was walking and saw rabbits all
                                                             over the place.'

1. WOW VERY-BIG AIRPORT, HAVE AIRPLANE MANY.   (IN-A-ROW)

2. BEFORE NONE, NOW HAVE DEAF BUSINESS MANY.   (ALL-OVER)

3. I LOOK-AT, SEE BIRD 5.   (IN-A-ROW)

4. ARMY READY, IT HAVE AIRPLANE 25.   (IN-A-ROW)

5. PARTY FINISH, WOW BEER CAN MANY.   (ALL-OVER)

6. NOW PRICE HIGH, CAR NEW MANY CAN'T SELL. (IN-A-ROW)

_____t_____

7. BEER CAN FATHER ENJOY COLLECT. THERE HOME HAVE 150. (IN-A-ROW)

Classifier: 1 Incorporating Number

The classifier CL:1 is used to show direction of movement of an upright human or animal. Note that the palm side of the CL:1 classifier represents the front of the human or animal.

EXAMPLES:

A. MAN CL:1-THERE-TO-HERE. 'The man came up to me.'

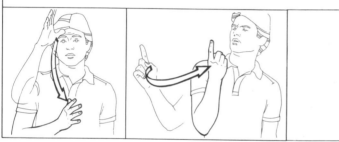

B. MAN CL:1-HERE-TO-THERE. 'The man walked away from me.'

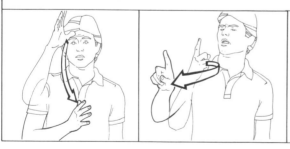

C. MAN CL:1-THERE-TO-THERE. 'The man walked by.'

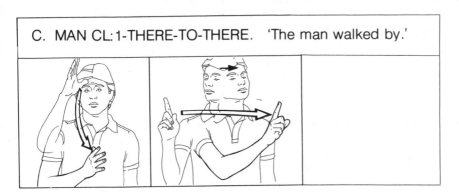

The CL:1 classifier can incorporate the numbers 1-5 to indicate the number of upright humans or animals in motion.

EXAMPLES:

D. CL:1(2)-THERE-TO-HERE BAWL-ME-OUT. 'The two of them came up to me and bawled me out.'

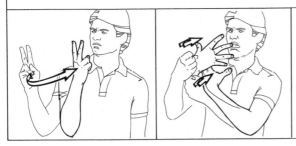

E. WOMAN CL:1(3)-THERE-TO-THERE. 'The three women passed by.'

Exercise 21.2:

Incorporate the number given in parentheses into the CL:1 classifier in the following sentences.

EXAMPLE:

STUDENT CL:1-THERE-TO-HERE COMPLAIN-REPEATEDLY.
'The student came up to me and complained.'
  (2)
     STUDENT CL:1(2)-THERE-TO-HERE COMPLAIN-REPEATEDLY.
     'The two students came up to me and complained.'

                _____ n _____
1. CL:1-THERE-TO-THERE, I SEE ~ NONE. (3)

2. GIRL CL:1-THERE-TO-HERE CHAT FINISH, CL:1-HERE-TO-THERE. (2)

3. BOY CL:1-THERE-TO-HERE, DEMAND MONEY. I SHOCK. (5)

4. BEAR CL:1-THERE-TO-HERE, I HERE-RUN-THERE. (2)

            _____ q _____ _____ whq _____
5. CAN I CL:1-HERE-TO-THERE, ASK-HIM TIME MEETING WHAT? (4)

NOTE: Other Uses of Classifier:1

The classifier CL:1 can use different movements to show actions of upright humans or animals.

'to pass by quickly'	'to saunter by'
	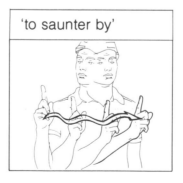

'to turn away'	'to stagger'

Both hands can form the CL:1 classifier to show action and the relative position of two or more upright humans or animals.

'to go up to another person or animal'	'the two of them go up to another person or animal'

'two of them follow another person or animal from behind'	'to approach a person, hesitate and walk away'
	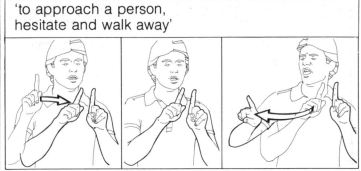

More Quantifiers

Some other classifiers which are used as quantifiers are:

CL:44	CL:B	CL:BB

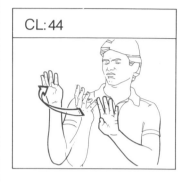 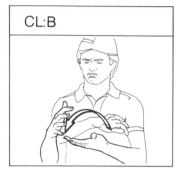 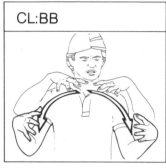

To mean many objects such as boyfriends, shirts, books.

To mean a small pile of objects such as dishes, food, homework.

To mean a large pile of objects such as clothes, furniture, many dishes.

These quantifiers may appear either before or after the noun, or at the end of the sentence.

EXAMPLES:

```
        ___t ___
A.  FOOD CL:B, HE LIKE HE.   'He likes a lot of food.'
```

```
   ___t ____
CL:B FOOD, HE LIKE HE.   'He likes a lot of food.'
_t ___
FOOD, HE LIKE CL:B HE.   'He likes a lot of food.'
```

Exercise 21.3:

Form responses to the following questions using the classifier given in parentheses.

EXAMPLE:

<u>   q   </u>

Question: SHE HAVE BOY FRIEND?   'Does she have a boyfriend?'
          (CL:44)

Response: SHE HAVE CL:44   'She has many.'
          CL:44 HAVE SHE.   'She has many.'

<u>   q   </u>
1. FOOD LEFT THERE?   (CL:B)

<u>   whq   </u>
2. FURNITURE YOU HAVE HOW-MUCH?   (CL:BB)

<u>   q   </u>
3. DIRTY CLOTHES YOU HAVE?   (CL:BB)

<u>   q   </u>
4. YOU TAKE MEAT FINISH YOU?   (CL:B)

<u>   q   </u>
5. SHE HAVE DRESS MANY?   (CL:44)

<u>   whq   </u>
6. HOW-MANY PEOPLE THEY WANT BUY TICKET?   (CL:44)

<u>   q   </u>
7. CLOTHES OLD, IT HAVE?   (CL:BB)

Vocabulary

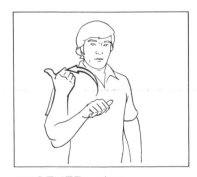

ANOTHER, other

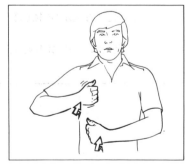

ARMY

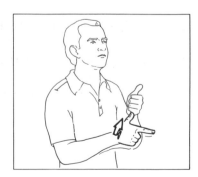

ASSISTANT

227

BEAR

BLUSH

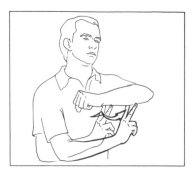

BRIDGE

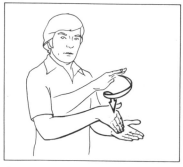

CENTER, middle

CHANNEL, knob

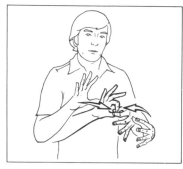

CONNECT, belong, join

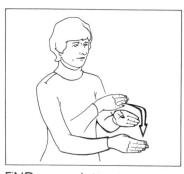

END, complete

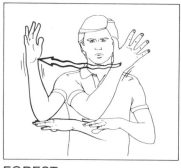

FOREST

GENERAL, broad

GOOD-AT, skilled, expert

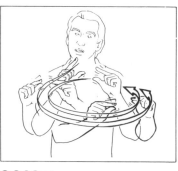

GOSSIP, rumor

HIGH

JUST, only

LINE

LOCK-UP

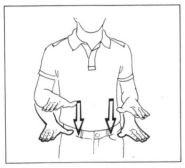
LOW, lower

MATCH, combine

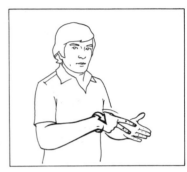
MEAN, meaning

MELT, dissolve, fade

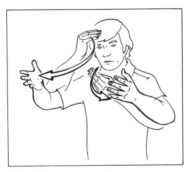
NEWS, information

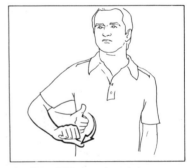
OPERATE (on body),
surgery

PAINT
Noun: paint

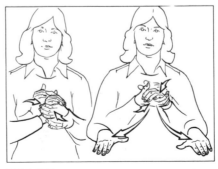
PEACE

PLUG-IN
Noun: plug

PRETEND, fool

SECRET, private,
confidential

SHOCK

SHOUT

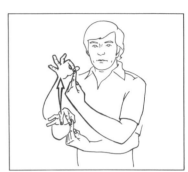

SPECIAL, except

SPIRIT, soul, ghost

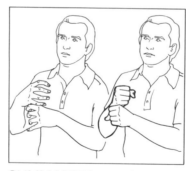

SUMMARIZE, condense,
abbreviate

SUPERVISE

TEMPT

TRADE-PLACES-WITH,
switch

WAR, battle

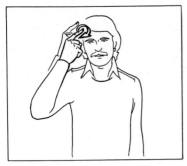

WONDER

LESSON 22

Outlining for Shape and Detail

The tips of the index fingers can be used to outline the shape of an object or to show detail of an object.

EXAMPLES:

A. HOME HAVE TABLE OUTLINE-KIDNEY-SHAPED.   'I have a table at home that is kidney-shaped.'

B. FLOWER BOWL HAVE SCALLOPED-RIM.   'The flower bowl has a scalloped rim.'

C. HAVE PAPER OUTLINE-RECTANGLE THERE.   'There's a big piece of paper there.'

Exercise 22.1:

Outline and give detail of the objects in the following pictures.

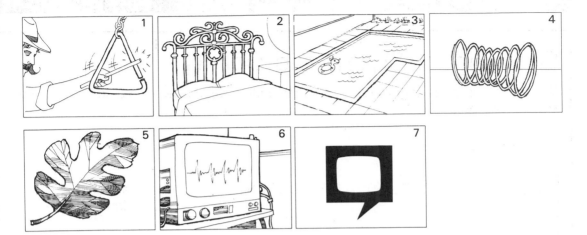

Shaping Objects With Classifier:BB

The classifier:CL:BB can be used to describe the surface shape of an object.

EXAMPLES:

A. BED OLD HAVE CL:BB-DIP.   'The old bed has a dip in the middle.'

B. GRASS CL:BB-SLOPE.   'The lawn has a gentle slope.'

C. NEW-YORK THERE HAVE BUILDING CL:BB-TALL-SIDES.
'New York has many tall buildings.'

Exercise 22.2:

Use the classifier:CL:BB to describe the surface shapes of the objects in the following pictures.

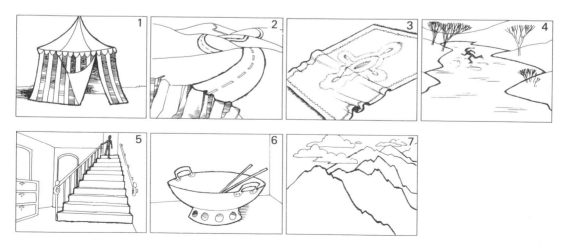

Classifiers Showing Motion

Some classifiers can be used to show the motion of the humans, animals, or objects they represent.

EXAMPLES:

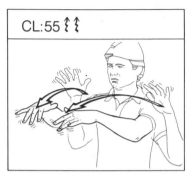

CL:55 ⭤

To mean a large quantity of people, cars, animals, etc., moving toward a specific location.

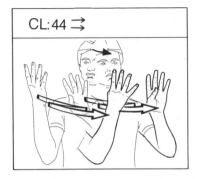

CL:44 ⭤

To mean a continuing stream of people or animals filing past.

CL:44 ⭤

To mean a continuing stream of objects filing along as on an assembly line such as newspapers on a conveyer belt.

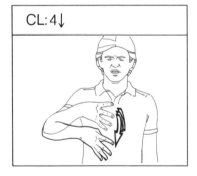

CL:4↓

To mean a flow of liquid such as a gas leak, a runny nose, running water, bleeding, etc.

EXAMPLES:

A. IT HAVE S-A-L-E PEOPLE CL:55↕↕   'People were rushing to the sale.'

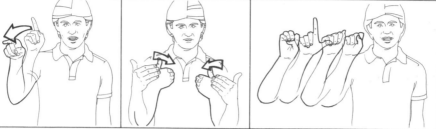

B. RESTAURANT PEOPLE CL:44 ⇉ IT GOOD IT.   'That restaurant is good, so
                                              many people go there.'
C. BEFORE WORK P-O, LETTER CL:44 ⇉ .   'I used to work at the post office
                                         sorting mail.'
D. WATER CL:4↓ GO-TO-IT FIX!   'The water's dripping, go fix it!'

Exercise 22.3:

Substitute each of the signs in the lists into the model sentence given.

EXAMPLE:

I SIT WATCH CHILDREN CL:44 ⇉ SCHOOL.
'I sat and watched the children going to school.'
   TEACHER
      I SIT WATCH TEACHER CL:44 ⇉ SCHOOL.
      'I sat and watched the teachers going to school.'

1. BEFORE I WORK FACTORY TOMATO CL:44⇉.
   COKE
   CAN
   FISH
   CAR

2. MEETING IMPORTANT PEOPLE CL:55⇅.
   DEAF
   COP
   INTERPRETER
   RESEARCHER

3. #BUSY HE DAILY PEOPLE CL:44 ⇒ HIS ROOM.
   STUDENT
   SICK PEOPLE
   ACTOR
   BOY, GIRL

4. AWFUL ALL-NIGHT WATER CL:4↓
   #GAS
   NOSE
   TOILET
   ROOF

Vocabulary

AFRICA

APPROACH

AUSTRALIA

BAPTIST, baptize

BLIND

BOWL

#BUSY

CANADA

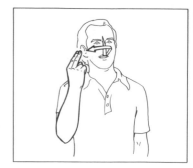

CATHOLIC

CHINA, Chinese

COMMUTE, go back and forth

CONGRATULATIONS

COOPERATE

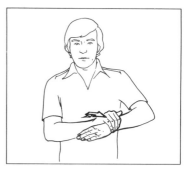

EGYPT

ENGLAND, British, English

EPISCOPAL

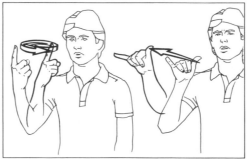

FOREVER

238

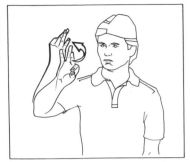

FRANCE, French

#GAS

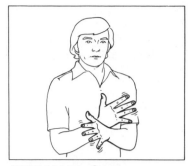

GERMANY, German

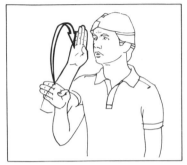

GOD

GRASS

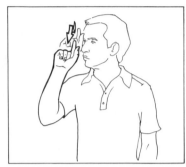

GREECE, Greek

HOSPITAL, infirmary

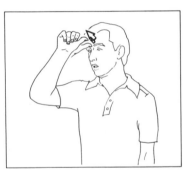

INDIA, Indian

ISRAEL, Jewish

ITALY

JAPAN, Japanese

LUTHERAN

239

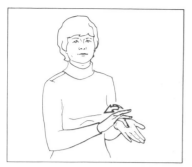  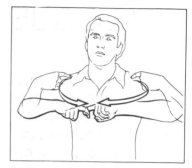

MEDICINE, chemical   METHODIST   MEXICO, Mexican

MORMON   NATIVE-AMERICAN, Indian   PROTESTANT

RELIGION, religious   ROOF   RUSSIA, Russian

 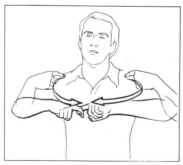 

SCOTLAND, Scottish   SPAIN, Spanish   TOMATO

DIALOGUE 7

Jack and Alice are discussing television decoders. These decoders, also known as closed caption decoders, are now a widespread fixture in many Deaf people's homes. These devices, when connected to a TV setup, make it possible to see subtitles on normal TV programming, much like watching subtitled foreign films. Most prime time and some daytime television is now closed captioned. Also, many video rentals have closed captions that can be seen using a decoder. Federal law now requires that new televisions be manufactured with a decoder chip built in so that no additional equipment will need to be purchased by the Deaf person to watch the captions.

Jack: I GET T-V CAPTION LAST-WEEK.   TRUE WONDERFUL.

Alice: I FINISH ORDER.   WAIT-CONTINUALLY, NOT-YET

            ___ whq _____
ARRIVE.   LOOK ~ LIKE WHAT?

Jack: CL:BB (flat) CL:BB (wide), METAL.   HAVE CL:F

        _____ if _____
CHANNEL.   SUPPOSE T-V NOW HAVE CAPTION, YOU O-N IT

C-A-P-T-I-O-N, FINISH IT T-V CAPTION.

Alice: THEY MAKE SEVERAL T-V CAPTION, WRONG PEOPLE

CL:55 ⇃⇂ WANT.   THEY NOT EXPECT.   NOW START MORE

Cl.:44 ⇉ SELL-REPEATEDLY.

             —rq—
Jack: T-V CAPTION WORK HOW?   WELL, T-V HAVE CL:G+++

(downward), 1 CL:G THAT-ONE IT LINE 21.   IT HAVE

CAPTION.   MUST HAVE BOX, THAT-ONE T-V CAPTION, PLUG-IN

FINISH, WILL IT APPEAR CAPTION.

Alice: TRUE WONDERFUL.   I HURRY GET.

halloween = < cut of eye   (raccoon w/ "r" into)

easter = e shake

Christmas = C curve around

Independence + Day

Marine = choking motion (one hand)

Navy = salute w/ N

Air Force ⎫
air planes ⎬ = I love you sign
air port ⎭

army / military = Two fists (holding rifle)

THE MANUAL ALPHABET

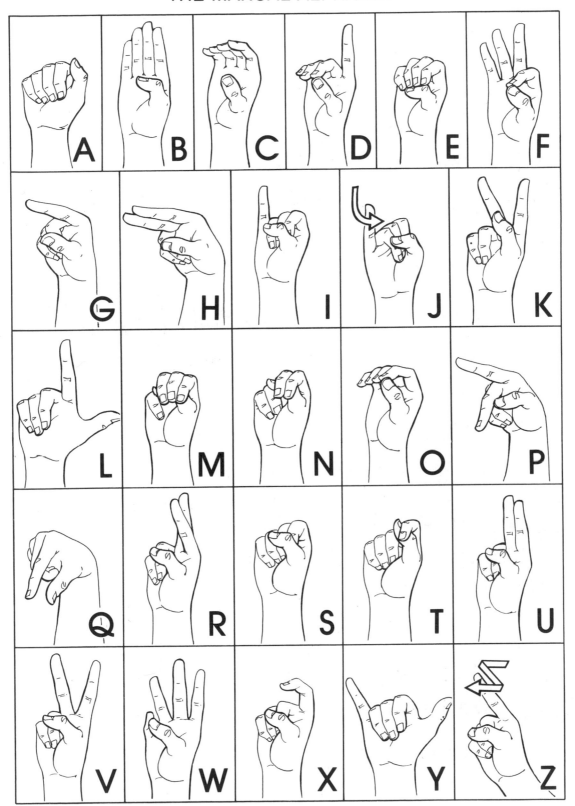

Japan ∠ >
China ㄱ on chest
Vietnam V middle to eye
Sinapore ○ with fingers
Canada fist to chest

golf
basketball
bowling
pool
bicycle : paddle
running : 2 pointers ∥ ground / hook them
diving : hands together
Soccer : palm to floor; hit w/ side of
hand
ski : ~~1~~ curled pointer to sky
skatting : 2
horsebackriding : horse +
backpacking : straps

football : ~~laces~~ fingers spread
loosely bound
wrestling : loosely linked
shake

NUMBERS

zero

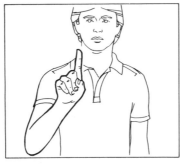

one

two

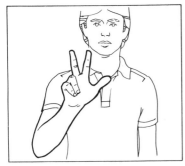

three

four

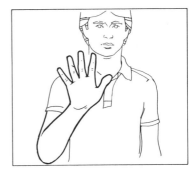

five

six

seven

eight

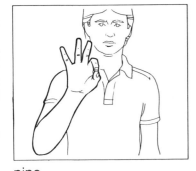

nine

ten

eleven

245

twelve

thirteen

fourteen

fifteen

sixteen

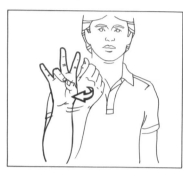

seventeen

eighteen

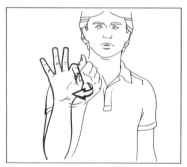

nineteen

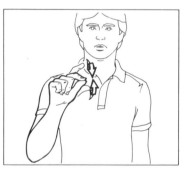

twenty

twenty-one

twenty-two

twenty-three

246

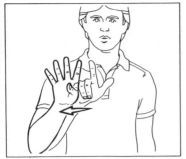 twenty-four

 twenty-five

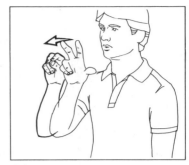 thirty

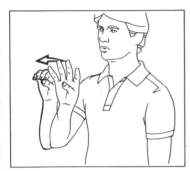 forty

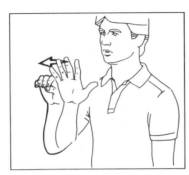 fifty

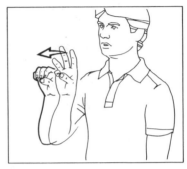 sixty

 seventy

 eighty

 ninety

 one hundred

 one thousand

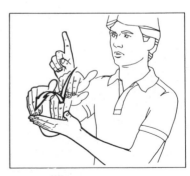 one million

REFERENCES

AMERICAN SIGN LANGUAGE

Baker, C. Regulators and Turn-taking in American Sign Language Discourse. In Friedman, L. (Ed.). *On the Other Hand: New Perspectives in American Sign Language.* New York: Academic Press. 1977.

Baker, C. and Cokely, D. *American Sign Language, A Teacher's Resource Text on Curriculum, Methods, and Evaluation.* Silver Spring, Maryland: T.J. Publishers, Inc. 1980.

Baker, C. and Cokely, D. *American Sign Language, A Teacher's Resource Text on Grammar and Culture.* Silver Spring, Maryland: T.J. Publishers, Inc. 1980.

Baker, C. and Padden, C. Focusing on the Nonmanual Components of American Sign Language. In Siple, P. (Ed.). *Understanding Language Through Sign Language Research.* New York: Academic Press. 1978.

Baker, C. and Padden, C. *American Sign Language: A Look at its History, Structure, and Community.* Silver Spring, Maryland: T.J. Publishers, Inc. 1978.

Baker, C. Sentences in American Sign Language. In Baker, C. and Battison, R. (Eds.). *Sign Language and the Deaf Community.* Silver Spring, Maryland: National Association of the Deaf. 1980.

Battison, R. *Lexical Borrowing in American Sign Language.* Silver Spring, Maryland: Linstok Press. 1978.

Battison, R. Signs Have Parts: A Simple Idea. In Baker, C. and Battison, R. (Eds.). *Sign Language and the Deaf Community.* Silver Spring, Maryland: National Association of the Deaf. 1980.

Bellugi, U. How Signs Express Complex Meanings. In Baker, C. and Battison, R. (Eds.). *Sign Language and the Deaf Community.* Silver Spring, Maryland: National Association of the Deaf. 1980.

Brill, R. G. (Ed.) *National Conference on Deaf and Hard of Hearing People Proceedings.* Silver Spring, MD: T.J. Publishers, 1989.

Eastman, G., Norestsky, M. and Censoplano, S. *From Mime To Sign.* Silver Spring, Maryland: T.J. Publishers, Inc. 1989.

Frishberg, N. Arbitrariness and Iconicity: Historical Change in American Sign Language. *Language,* 51:676–710. 1975.

Humphries, T., Padden, C., and O'Rourke, T.J. *Un Curso Basico De Lenguaje Americano De Senas.* Translated by Lourdes Rubio. Edited by Gilbert L. Delgado. Silver Spring, Maryland: T.J. Publishers, 1991.

Klima, E. and Bellugi, U. *The Signs of Language.* Cambridge, Massachusetts: Harvard University Press. 1979.

Kyle, J. and Woll, B. (Eds.). *Language in Sign: An International Perspective on Sign Language.* London: Croom Helm. 1983.

Lane, H. *When the Mind Hears: A History of the Deaf.* New York: Random House, 1984.

Lane, H. *The Deaf Experience: Classics in Language and Education.* Cambridge, Massachusetts: Harvard Press. 1984.

Lane, H. and Grosjean, F. (Eds.). *Recent Perspectives in ASL.* Hillsdale, NJ: Erlbaum. 1980.

Liddell, S. Nonmanual Signals and Relative Clauses in American Sign Language. In Siple, P. (Ed.). *Understanding Language Through Sign Language Research.* New York: Academic Press. 1978.

O'Rourke, T.J., *A Basic Vocabulary.* Introduction by Ursula Belugi. Silver Spring, Maryland: T.J. Publishers, Inc. 1978.

O'Rourke, T.J. (Ed.) Psycholinguistics and Total Communication: The State of the Art. Silver Spring, MD: *American Annals of the Deaf, 1972.*

Padden, C. *American Sign Language.* In Van Cleve, J. (Ed.). *Encyclopedia of Deaf People and Deafness.* 1986.

Padden, C. *The Interaction of Morphology and Syntax in American Sign Language.* Outstanding Dissertations in Linguistics, Series IV. New York: Garland Press. 1988.

Perlmutter, D. The Language of the Deaf. *New York Review of Books* (March 28, 1991). New York: New York Review of Books. 1991.

Spradley, T. and Spradley, J. *Deaf Like Me.* New York: Random House. 1978.

Sternberg, M. *American Sign Language—A Comprehensive Dictionary.* New York: Harper and Row. 1981.

Sternberg, M. *American Sign Language Concise Dictionary.* New York: Harper and Row. 1990.

Sternberg, M. *American Sign Language Dictionary.* New York: Harper and Row. 1987.

Stokoe, W., Casterline, D., and Croneberg, C. *A Dictionary of American Sign Language on Linguistic Principles.* Silver Spring, Maryland: Linstok Press. 1976.

Supalla, S. *The Book of Name Signs: Naming in American Sign Language.* San Diego, CA: Dawn Sign Press. 1992.

Supalla, T. and Newport, E. How Many Seats in A Chair? The Derivation of Nouns and Verbs in American Sign Language. In Siple, P. (Ed.). *Understanding Language Through Sign Language Research.* New York: Academic Press. 1978.

Valli, C. and Lucas, C. *Linguistics of American Sign Language.* Washington, DC: Gallaudet University Press. 1992.

Volterra, V. and Stokoe, W. *Sign Language Research '83; Proceedings of the III International Symposium on Sign Language Research, Rome, 1983.* Silver Spring, Maryland: Linstok Press. 1985.

Wilbur, R. *American Sign Language and Sign Systems.* Baltimore: University Park Press. 1979.

Woodward, J. Black Southern Signing. *Language in Society,* 5:303–311. 1976.

Woodward, J. *How You Gonna Get to Heaven If You Can't Talk to Jesus?: On Depathologizing Deafness.* Silver Spring, MD: T.J. Publishers, Inc. 1982.

Woodward, J. *Signs of Sexual Behavior.* Silver Spring, MD: T.J. Publishers, Inc. 1979.

Woodward, J. *Signs of Drug Use.* Silver Spring, MD: T.J. Publishers, Inc. 1981.

Woodward, J. and Erting, C. Synchronic Variation and Historical Change in American Sign Language. *Language Sciences.* 37:9–12. 1974.

DEAF COMMUNITY AND DEAF CULTURE

Becker, G. *Growing Old in Silence.* Berkeley: University of California Press. 1980.

Bowe, F. *Changing the Rules.* Silver Spring, Maryland: T.J. Publishers, Inc. 1986.

Bragg, B. and Bergman, E. *Tales from a Clubroom.* Washington, DC: Gallaudet University Press. 1981.

Bullard, D. *Islay.* Silver Spring, Maryland: T.J. Publishers, Inc. 1986.

Crouch, B. A Deaf Commonwealth. In Van Cleve, J. (Ed.). *Encyclopedia of Deaf People and Deafness.* New York: McGraw-Hill. 1986.

DeBee, J. (Producer). *The LACD Story.* Los Angeles: Beyond Sound. 1985.

Delgado, G., editor. *The Hispanic Deaf: Issues and Bilingual Challenges for Special Education.* Washington, D.C.: Gallaudet University Press. 1984.

Eastman, G. *Sign Me Alice.* Washington, DC: Gallaudet College Press. 1975.

Erting, C. Cultural Conflict in a School for Deaf Children. Anthropology and Education Quarterly. 16:225–243. 1985.

Gannon, J. *Deaf Heritage—A Narrative History of Deaf America.* Washington, D.C.: National Association of the Deaf. 1980.

Gannon, J., *The Week the World Heard Gallaudet.* Washington, D.C.: Gallaudet University Press. 1989.

Graybill, P. (Performer). *Poetry in Motion.* College Park, MD: Sign Media, Inc. 1991.

Groce, N.E. *Everybody Here Spoke Sign Language: Hereditary Deafness on Martha's Vineyard.* Cambridge, MA: Harvard University Press, 1985.

Higgins, P. *Outsiders in a Hearing World.* Beverly Hills, CA: Sage Publications. 1980.

Holcomb, M. and Wood, S. *Deaf Women: A Parade Through the Decades.* Berkeley, California: Dawn Sign Press. 1988.

Humphries, T. Deaf Culture and Cultures. In *Multicultural Issues in Deafness.* In K. Christensen and G. Delgado, (Eds.). New York: Longman Press. 1993.

Humphries, T. An Introduction to the Culture of Deaf People in the United States: Content Notes & Reference Material for Teachers. *Sign Language Studies,* 72:209–240. 1992.

Jacobs, L. *A Deaf Adult Speaks Out.* Washington, D.C.: Gallaudet College Press. 1980.

Kannapell, B. Personal Awareness and Advocacy in the Deaf Community. In Baker, C. and Battison, R. (Eds.). *Sign Language and the Deaf Community.* Silver Spring, Maryland: National Association of the Deaf. 1980.

Lane, H. *When the Mind Hears: A History of the Deaf.* New York: Random House. 1984.

Lane, H. *The Mask of Benevolence: Disabling the Deaf Community.* New York: Alfred A. Knopf. 1992.

Lane, H. *The Wild Boy of Aveyron.* Cambridge, Massachusetts: Harvard University Press. 1976.

Meadow, K. 1972. Sociolinguistics, Sign Language, and the Deaf Subculture. In O'Rourke, T.J. (Ed.). *Psycholinguistics and Total Communication: The State of the Art.* Silver Spring, Maryland: National Association of the Deaf. 1972.

Neisser, A. *The Other Side of Silence: Sign Language and the Deaf Community in America.* Washington, D.C.: Gallaudet University Press. 1990.

Padden, C., and Humphries, T. *Deaf in America: Voices From a Culture.* Cambridge, Massachusetts: Harvard University Press. 1988.

Padden, C. and Markowicz, H. Cultural Conflicts Between Hearing and Deaf Communities. In *Proceedings of the Seventh World Congress of the World Federation of the Deaf.* Silver Spring, Maryland: National Association of the Deaf. 1976.

Padden, C. The Deaf Community and the Culture of Deaf People. In Baker, C. and Battison, R. (Eds.). *Sign Language and the Deaf Community.* Silver Spring, Maryland: National Association of the Deaf. 1980.

Rutherford, S. Funny in Deaf—Not in Hearing. *Journal of American Folklore,* 96:310–322. 1983.

Sacks, O. *Seeing Voices: A Journey in the World of the Deaf.* Berkeley, California: University of California Press. 1989.

Schein, J. *At Home Among Strangers.* Washington, D.C.: Gallaudet University Press. 1989.

Stokoe, W., editor. *American Deaf Culture: An Anthology.* Silver Spring, Maryland: Linstok Press. 1989.

Stokoe, W., editor. *Sign and Culture: A Reader For Students of American Sign Language.* Silver Spring, Maryland: Linstok Press. 1985.

Supalla, T. (Producer). *Charles Krauel: Profile of a Deaf Filmmaker.* Film. San Diego, CA: Dawn Sign Press. 1992.

Valli, C. (Performer). *Poetry in Motion.* College Park, MD: Sign Media, Inc. 1991.

Van Cleve, J. and Crouch, B. *A Place of Their Own: Creating the Deaf Community in America.* Washington, D.C.: Gallaudet University Press. 1989.

Woodward, J. Historical Bases of American Sign Language. In Siple, P. (Ed.). *Understanding Language Through Sign Language Research.* New York: Academic Press. 1978.

Woodward, J. Sociolinguistic Research on American Sign Language: A Historical Perspective. In Baker, C. and Battison, R. (Eds.). *Sign Language and the Deaf Community.* Silver Spring, Maryland: National Association of the Deaf. 1980.

ANSWER KEY

EXERCISE 1.1

1. YOU-PL.
2. THEY
3. I
4. HE/SHE/IT
5. THEY
6. YOU
7. THEY
8. WE

EXERCISE 1.2

1. YOU TALL YOU. 'You are tall.'
2. IT HEAVY IT. 'It is heavy.'
3. I SURPRISED I. 'I am surprised.'
4. THEY DEAF THEY. 'They are deaf.'
5. YOU HEARING YOU. 'You are hearing.'
6. I MAD I. 'I am mad.'
7. SHE SLEEPY SHE. 'She is sleepy.'
8. WE DEAF WE. 'We are deaf.'
9. IT LIGHT IT. 'It is light.'
10. YOU HAPPY YOU. 'You are happy.'
11. WE SURPRISED WE. 'We are surprised.'
12. HE INTERESTING HE. 'He is interesting.'
13. YOU PRETTY YOU. 'You are pretty.'
14. IT UGLY IT. 'It is ugly.'
15. I SHORT I. 'I am short.'
16. THEY SURPRISED THEY. 'They are surprised.'
17. IT BIG IT. 'It is big.'
18. I SLEEPY I. 'I am sleepy.'
19. IT SMALL IT. 'It is small.'
20. SHE DEAF SHE. 'She is deaf.'

EXERCISE 2.1

1. YOUR
2. HER
3. OUR
4. THEIR
5. YOUR-PL.
6. ITS
7. MY
8. HIS
9. HIS
10. THEIR

EXERCISE 2.2

1. SHE MY SISTER. 'She is my sister.'
2. HE MY BROTHER. 'He is my brother.'

251

3. HE YOUR FATHER. 'He is your father.'
4. HE OUR FATHER. 'He is our father.'
5. SHE MY GRANDMOTHER 'She is my grandmother.'
6. HE MY FRIEND. 'He is my friend.'
7. HE YOUR GRANDFATHER. 'He is your grandfather.'
8. HE YOUR TEACHER. 'He is your teacher.'
9. HE MY STUDENT. 'He is my student.'
10. HE MY FRIEND. 'He is my friend.'
11. HE BOY. 'He is a boy.'
12. SHE GIRL. 'She is a girl.'
13. HE MAN. 'He is a man.'
14. SHE WOMAN. 'She is a woman.'

EXERCISE 2.3

1. SHE HER SISTER SHE. 'She is her sister.'
2. SHE HER MOTHER SHE. 'She is her mother.'
3. SHE THEIR TEACHER SHE. 'She is their teacher.'
4. SHE HIS GRANDMOTHER SHE. 'She is his grandmother.'
5. HE HER FRIEND HE. 'He is her friend.'
6. HE HIS STUDENT HE. 'He is his student.'
7, HE HER BROTHER HE. 'He is her brother.'
8. HE HIS FATHER HE. 'He is his father.'
9. HE HER GRANDFATHER HE. 'He is her grandfather.'
10. SHE HIS SISTER SHE. 'She is his sister.'

EXERCISE 3.1

1. I FORGET BOOK I. 'I forgot a book.'
2. I REMEMBER BOOK I. 'I remember the book.'
3. I LIKE BOOK I. 'I like the book.'
4. I KNOW BOOK I. 'I know the book.'
5. I WANT BOOK I. 'I want a book.'
6. I HAVE BOOK I. 'I have a book.'
7. I READ BOOK I. 'I read a book.'
8. I LOSE BOOK I. 'I lost the book.'
9. I FIND BOOK I. 'I found a book.'
10. I ENJOY BOOK I. 'I enjoyed the book.'

EXERCISE 3.2

1. WOMAN SHE REMEMBER BOOK SHE. 'The woman remembers the book.'
2. WOMAN SHE REMEMBER YOUR NAME SHE. 'The woman remembers your name.'
3. WOMAN SHE FORGET YOUR NAME SHE. 'The woman forgot your name.'
4. WOMAN SHE FORGET YOUR BOOK SHE. 'The woman forgot your book.'
5. BOY HE FORGET YOUR BOOK HE. 'The boy forgot your book.'
6. BOY HE HAVE YOUR BOOK HE. 'The boy has your book.'
7. BOY HE HAVE YOUR PAPER HE. 'The boy has your paper.'
8. BOY HE NEED YOUR PAPER HE. 'The boy needs your paper.'
9. GIRL SHE NEED YOUR PAPER SHE. 'The girl needs your paper.'
10. GIRL SHE REMEMBER SIGN SHE. 'The girl remembers signs.'
11. MAN HE REMEMBER SIGN HE. 'The man remembers signs.'
12. MAN HE PRACTICE SIGN HE. 'The man practices signs.'
13. WOMAN SHE PRACTICE SIGN SHE. 'The woman practices signs.'
14. WOMAN SHE HAVE CHAIR SHE. 'The woman has a chair.'
15. WOMAN SHE NEED CHAIR SHE. 'The woman needs a chair.'

16. WOMAN SHE NEED CAR SHE.   'The woman needs a car.'
17. MAN HE NEED MONEY HE.   'The man needs money.'
18. MAN HE WANT MONEY HE.   'The man wants money.'
19. GIRL SHE WANT BOOK SHE.   'The girl wants a book.'
20. GIRL SHE HAVE BOOK SHE.   'The girl has a book.'

EXERCISE 3.3

1. I READ BOOK INTERESTING.   'I read an interesting book.'
2. HE HAVE HOME PRETTY HE.   'He has a pretty home.'
3. SHE WANT CHAIR BLUE.   'She wants a blue chair.'
4. I REMEMBER MAN TALL.   'I remember the tall man.'
5. HE LOSE BOOK GREEN HE.   'He lost a green book.'
6. THEY FIND BOX SMALL.   'They found a small box.'
7. HE WANT TABLE NEW.   'He wants a new table.'
8. I NEED PAPER YELLOW FOR CLASS I.   'I need yellow paper for class.'
9. I KNOW WOMAN DEAF I.   'I know a deaf woman.'
10. SHE LIKE CAR SMALL SHE.   'She likes the small car.'

EXERCISE 3.4

1. I READ INTERESTING BOOK.   'I read an interesting book.'
2. HE HAVE PRETTY HOME HE.   'He has a pretty home.'
3. SHE WANT BLUE CHAIR.   'She wants a blue chair.'
4. I REMEMBER TALL MAN.   'I remember the tall man.'
5. HE LOSE GREEN BOOK HE.   'He lost a green book.'
6. THEY FIND SMALL BOX.   'They found a small box.'
7. HE WANT NEW TABLE.   'He wants a new table.'
8. I NEED YELLOW PAPER FOR CLASS I.   'I need yellow paper for class.'
9. I KNOW DEAF WOMAN I.   'I know a deaf woman.'
10. SHE LIKE SMALL CAR SHE.   'She likes the small car.'

EXERCISE 3.5

1. IT CL:BB.   'It is long and flat.'
2. IT CL:ÏL.   'It is large, flat and round.'
3. IT CL:F.   'It is small, flat and round.'
4. IT CL:BB.   'It is long and flat.'
5. IT CL:BB.   'It is long and flat.'
6. IT CL:ÏL.   'It is quite large, flat and round.'
7. IT CL:C.   'It is small and container-like.'
8. IT CL:ÏL.   'It is quite large, flat and round.'
9. IT CL:CC.   'It is quite large and container-like.'
10. IT CL:ÏL.   'It is flat and round.'
11. IT CL:CC.   'It is large and container-like.'
12. IT CL:F.   'It is small, flat and round.'

EXERCISE 4.1

————————n————————
1. HE DON'T-LIKE MOVIE HE.   'He doesn't like the movie.'
————————————n————————————————
2. DAUGHTER SHE DON'T-LIKE SCHOOL SHE.   'My daughter doesn't like school.'
——————n————————
3 I NOT SEE DOG I.   'I don't see a dog.'

253

                       _____n_____
4. IT SMELL GOOD NOT IT.   'It doesn't smell good.'
              _____n_____
5. I NOT UNDERSTAND BOOK I.   'I don't understand the book.'
              _____n_____
6. THEY BELIEVE YOU NOT.   'They don't believe you.'
              _____n_____
7. CAT IT NOT HUNGRY IT.   'The cat isn't hungry.'
              _____n_____
8. HOUSE IT NOT EXPENSIVE IT.   'The house is not expensive.'
              _____n_____
9. IT FOOD HOT NOT IT.   'The food is not hot.'
              _____n_____
10. WOMAN SHE DON'T-WANT T-T-Y SHE.   'The woman doesn't want a TTY.'
              _____n_____
11. SHE DON'T-KNOW SIGN SHE.   'The woman doesn't know sign language.'
              _____n_____
12. BOY HE LOSE MONEY NOT HE.   'The boy didn't lose the money.'
              _____n_____
13. CAR IT BLUE NOT IT.   'The car isn't blue.'

EXERCISE 4.2

    __n____
1. I TIRED I.   'I'm not tired.'
    _____n_____
2. YOU UNDERSTAND ME.   'You don't understand me.'
    _____n_____
3. GIRL HAVE BOOK SHE.   'The girl doesn't have the book.'
    _____n_____
4. MY SISTER FIND MONEY.   'My sister didn't find the money.'
    _____n_____
5. I SMELL IT I.   'I don't smell it.'
    ____n___
6. I WORK I.   'I don't work.'
    _____n_____
7. THEY PRACTICE SIGN.   'They don't practice signs.'

EXERCISE 4.3

    _____q_____
1. HE LIKE WORK HE?   'Does he like to work?'
    _____q_____
2. TEACHER LOSE MY PAPER?   'Did the teacher lose my paper?'
    _____q_____
3. IT HOUSE COLD IT?   'Is the house cold?'
    _____q_____
4. GRANDMOTHER FIND MONEY?   'Did Grandmother find the money?'
    _____q_____
5. IT CAT HUNGRY IT?   'Is the cat hungry?'
    _____q_____
6. IT BOOK RIGHT IT?   'Is the book right?'
    _____q_____
7. DOG IT UNDERSTAND SIGN IT?   'Does the dog understand signs?'
    _____q_____
8. SHE KNOW MY NAME SHE?   'Does she know my name?'

_____ q _____
9. BOY HE SHORT HE? 'Is the boy short?'

_____ q _____
10. HE HEARING HE? 'Is he hearing?'

EXERCISE 4.4

_____ n _____
1. NO, HE DON'T-LIKE HE. 'No, he doesn't.'

_____ n _____
2. NO, HE NOT LOSE. 'No, he didn't.'

_____ y _____
3. YES, IT COLD IT. 'Yes, it is.'

_____ y _____
4. YES, SHE FIND. 'Yes, she did.'

_____ n _____
5. NO, IT NOT SICK IT. 'No, it isn't.'

_____ n ____
6. NO, IT NOT IT. 'No, it isn't.'

_____ y _____
7. YES, IT UNDERSTAND IT. 'Yes, it does.'

_____ y _____
8. YES, SHE KNOW SHE. 'Yes, she does.'

_____ y _____
9. YES, HE HEARING HE. 'Yes, he is.'

_____ n _____
10. NO, HE NOT HE. 'No, he's not.'

EXERCISE 4.5

_____ nq _____
1. YOU UNDERSTAND ME? 'You don't understand me?'

_____ nq _____
2. SHE SEE MOVIE NOT? 'She didn't see the movie?'

_____ nq _____
3. HE DEAF HE? 'He's not deaf?'

_____ nq _____
4. SHE DON'T-WANT CAT? 'She doesn't want the cat?'

_____ nq _____
5. HE DON'T-KNOW MY SISTER HE? 'He doesn't know my sister?'

_____ nq ___
6. IT DIRTY NOT IT? 'It's not dirty?'

_____ nq _____
7. HE NOT AMERICAN HE? 'He's not an American?'

DIALOGUE 1

Jack: Hello. Is she a friend of yours?
Tom: Yes. Her name is Betty Smith. She's from Indiana.
Jack: I'm happy to meet you. My name is Jack Jones. I'm from Minnesota.
Betty: I'm happy to meet you. Do you have a brother named Bob Jones?
Jack: Yes. Do you know him?
Betty: Yes, I know him.
Tom: Well, the deaf world is a small one!

EXERCISE 5.1

1. YESTERDAY I PRACTICE SIGN I.   'Yesterday I practiced my signs.'
2. RECENTLY HE BUY CAR HE.   'Recently, he bought a car.'
3. BEFORE BOY HE STUDENT HE.   'The boy was a student before.'
4. YESTERDAY SHE DIE SHE, SORRY.   'She died yesterday. I was sorry about it.'
5. LONG-AGO I TEACH RESIDENTIAL-SCHOOL I.   'I taught at a residential school a long time ago.'
6. RECENTLY WOMAN SHE LOSE P-I-N CL:F.   'Recently, the woman lost a round pin.'
   _____ n _____
7. YESTERDAY I NOT READ YOUR HOMEWORK.   'I didn't read your homework yesterday.'
8. RECENTLY HE LEARN SIGN HE.   'He learned sign language recently.'
9. BEFORE SHE HEARING SCHOOL.   'She went to a hearing school before.'
10. LONG-AGO SHE VISIT WASHINGTON SHE.   'She visited Washington a long time ago.'

EXERCISE 5.2

1. HE FATHER FINISH MAKE COOKIE HE.   'Father made cookies.'
2. SHE WRITE PAPER FINISH SHE.   'She wrote a paper.'
3. BROTHER FINISH READ BOOK HE.   'My brother has read the book.'
4. I FINISH SELL HOUSE I.   'I already sold the house.'
5. MOVIE I SEE FINISH I.   'I have seen the movie.'
6. I FINISH VISIT GRANDMOTHER I.   'I already visited Grandmother.'
7. MY SIGN FINISH IMPROVE.   'My sign language has already improved.'
8. HE FINISH DRINK WATER HE.   'He drank some water.'
9. SON HE GROW-UP FINISH HE.   'My son has grown up.'
10. I FINISH COOK ALL-DAY.   'I cooked all day.'

EXERCISE 5.3

1. TOMORROW I PRACTICE SIGN I.   'Tomorrow I will practice my signs.'
2. I WILL GO COLLEGE I.   'I will go to college.'
3. LATER I TO-TELEPHONE YOU I.   'I will telephone you later.'
4. HE LEARN SIGN WILL HE.   'He will learn sign language.'
5. COOKIE CL:ĻĻ I FUTURE MAKE I.   'I'll make a large cookie later on.'
6. AFTER-AWHILE T-T-Y SHE BUY SHE.   'After awhile, she will buy a TTY.'
7. TOMORROW I SEE MOVIE I.   'I'll see the movie tomorrow.'
8. PANTS I WILL WEAR I.   'I'll wear pants.'
9. MOTHER WILL STAY 1-WEEK.   'Mother will stay one week.'

EXERCISE 6.1

   _t _
1. TEA I PREFER I.   'I prefer tea.'
   _t _
2. TEA I HATE I.   'I hate tea.'
   ___t _
3. WORK I HATE I.   'I hate work.'
   ___t _
4. WORK I ENJOY I.   'I enjoy work.'
   _t _
5. T-V I ENJOY I.   'I enjoy TV.'
   _t _
6. T-V I LOOK-AT I.   'I watch TV.'
   ___t ___
7. BICYCLE I LOOK-AT I.   'I looked at the bicycle.'

    __ t ___
8. BICYCLE I DON'T-LIKE I.   'I don't like the bicycle.'
    __ t _
9. MEAT I DON'T-LIKE I.   'I don't like meat.'
    __ t _
10. MEAT I NOT EAT I.   'I don't eat meat.
    __ t __
11. SWEET I NOT EAT I.   'I don't eat sweets.'
    __ t __
12. SWEET I NOT BUY I.   'I don't buy sweets.'

EXERCISE 6.2

    __ t __
1. TICKET TOMORROW YOU-PAY-ME.   'I'll pay you for the ticket tomorrow.'
    __ t __
2. LETTER LATER YOU-SEND-ME. 'You send me the letter later.'
    _____ t _____
3. RIGHT ADDRESS TOMORROW YOU-TELL-ME.   'You tell me the right address tomorrow.'
    _____ t _____
4. TELETYPEWRITER NEW YOU-SHOW-ME WILL YOU.   'You will show me the new teletypewriter.'
5. YOU FINISH YOU-ASK-ME.   'You already asked me.'
    __ t __
6. LETTER YOU-HELP-ME WRITE WILL YOU.   'You will help me write the letter.'
7. YOU-GIVE-ME PICTURE NOW.   'You give me the picture now.'
8. AFTER-AWHILE YOU AGAIN YOU-ASK-ME.   'You ask me again after awhile.'
    _____ t _____
9. PRETTY CL:LL YOU-SHOW-ME WILL YOU.   'You will show me the pretty plate.'
    ____ t ____
10. UMBRELLA LONG-AGO YOU-GIVE-ME.   'You gave me the umbrella a long time ago.'

EXERCISE 6.3

1. YESTERDAY SHE-TELL-ME STAY.   'Yesterday she told me to stay.'
    __ t ___
2. CLOTHES TOMORROW HE-HELP-ME BUY.   'He will help me buy clothes tomorrow.'
3. FINISH HE-ASK-ME WAIT.   'He already asked me to wait.'
    __ t _
4. MOVIE LATER SHE-SHOW-ME.   'She will show me the movie later.'
    __ t __
5. MONEY TOMORROW SHE-SEND-IT.   'She will send them (the company) money tomorrow.'
    _____ q _____
6. WILL HE-ASK-YOU WORK?   'Will he ask you to work?'
    _____ q _____
7. BREAD TODAY HE-HELP-YOU MAKE?   'Will he help you make bread today?'
    _____ t _____
8. NEW WRISTWATCH HE-SHOW-YOU NOW.   'He will show you the new watch now.'
    _ t _
9. BOX SHE-SEND-YOU LATER.   'She will send you the box later.'

EXERCISE 6.4

    _ t _
1. BOX GIVE-CL:C↑-YOU.   'I'll give you a box.'
    __ t __
2. PAPER GIVE-CL:C↑-YOU.   'I'll give you a stack of paper.'

    — t —
3. WATER GIVE-CL:C-YOU. 'I'll give you a glass of water.'
    — t —
4. BOOK GIVE-CL:C↑-YOU. 'I'll give you a book.'
    — t —
5. GLASS GIVE-CL:C-YOU. 'I'll give you a glass.'
    — t —
6. BOTTLE GIVE-CL:C-YOU. 'I'll give you a bottle.'
    — t —
7. PLANT GIVE-CL:C-YOU. 'I'll give you a potted plant.'
    — t —
8. COKE GIVE-CL:C-YOU. 'I'll give you a coke.'

EXERCISE 7.1

1. TOMORROW YOU-GIVE-ME MONEY! 'Give me the money tomorrow!'
    — t —
2. LETTER YOU-SEND-HER MOTHER! 'Send Mother a letter!'
    — t —
3. T-T-Y BUY YOU! 'Buy a TTY!'
4. PRACTICE SIGN YOU! 'Practice signing!'
5. REMEMBER SIGN YOU! 'Remember the signs!'
6. TOMORROW AGAIN YOU-TELL-HER! 'Tell her again tomorrow!'
7. ADVERTISEMENT YOU-SEND-ME! 'Send me the advertisement!'
8. PAY-ATTENTION YOU! 'Pay attention!'

EXERCISE 7.2

1. I FIND 3 GLASS. 'I found 3 glasses.'
2. I FIND COAT 1. 'I found 1 coat.'
3. I FIND 5 PENCIL. 'I found 5 pencils.'
4. I FIND STAMP 2. 'I found 2 stamps.'
5. I FIND 4 KNIFE. 'I found 4 knives.'
6. I FIND SPOON 3. 'I found 3 spoons.'
7. TOMORROW BROTHER OLD 4. 'Tomorrow my brother will be 4 years old.'
8. TOMORROW BROTHER OLD 9. 'Tomorrow my brother will be 9 years old.'
9. TOMORROW BROTHER OLD 6. 'Tomorrow my brother will be 6 years old.'
10. TOMORROW BROTHER OLD 2. 'Tomorrow my brother will be 2 years old.'
11. TOMORROW BROTHER OLD 5. 'Tomorrow my brother will be 5 years old.'
12. TOMORROW BROTHER OLD 1. 'Tomorrow my brother will be 1 year old.'
13. FRIEND WILL SHE-MEET-ME TIME 9. 'My friend will meet me at 9 o'clock.'
14. FRIEND WILL SHE-MEET-ME TIME 8. 'My friend will meet me at 8 o'clock.'
15. FRIEND WILL SHE-MEET-ME TIME 4. 'My friend will meet me at 4 o'clock.'
16. FRIEND WILL SHE-MEET-ME TIME 6. 'My friend will meet me at 6 o'clock.'
17. FRIEND WILL SHE-MEET-ME TIME 1. 'My friend will meet me at 1 o'clock.'
18. FRIEND WILL SHE-MEET-ME TIME 7. 'My friend will meet me at 7 o'clock.'

EXERCISE 7.3

1. THREE-OF-US PLAN GO-AWAY. 'We (the three of us) plan to go.'
2. FIVE-OF-US PLAN GO-AWAY. 'We (the five of us) plan to go.'
3. TWO-OF-YOU PLAN GO-AWAY. 'You (the two of you) plan to go.'
4. FOUR-OF-US PLAN GO-AWAY. 'We (the four of us) plan to go.'
5. FIVE-OF-THEM GO-WITH WILL. 'They (the five of them) will go together.'
6. FOUR-OF-US GO-WITH WILL. 'We (the four of us) will go together.'
7. TWO-OF-THEM GO-WITH WILL. 'They (the two of them) will go together.'
8. THREE-OF-YOU GO-WITH WILL. 'You (the three of you) will go together.'

258

EXERCISE 7.4

1. HE GROW-UP RABBIT 10 HE.   'He raised 10 rabbits.'
2. SON HE NEED PANTS MANY HE.   'My son needs many pairs of pants.'
3. SHE ORDER HAMBURGER 2 SHE.   'She ordered 2 hamburgers.'
4. I ORDER FRENCH-FRIES 3 I.   'I ordered 3 french fries.'
5. IT STORE HAVE SHOES MANY IT.   'The store has many pairs of shoes.'
6. STUDENT HE HAVE MISTAKE A-FEW HE.   'The student has a few mistakes.'
7. SHE FINISH SHE-GIVE-ME PICTURE SEVERAL.   'She gave me several pictures.'
8. I FINISH I-MEET-HER NEW NEIGHBOR SEVERAL.   'I have met several new neighbors.'
   _____ n _____
9. TWO-OF-THEM NOT HAVE FRIEND MANY.   'They don't have many friends.'
10. PEOPLE A-FEW STILL WAIT.   'A few people are still waiting.'

DIALOGUE 2

Jack: Do you know my brother?
Betty: Yes, I have met him. My sister and your brother are good friends.
Jack: I didn't know your sister is Deaf.
Betty: She is Deaf. Her name is Mary Williams.
Jack: I'm surprised. I know her. The last time I saw her was six years ago.
Betty: I have many pictures of Mary. I will give some to you.
Jack: Fine. I want to see them.

EXERCISE 8.1

    _____ whq _____
1. ARRIVE YESTERDAY WHAT?   'What arrived yesterday?'
   _____ whq _____
   T-T-Y ARRIVE WHEN?   'When did the TTY arrive?'
   _____whq _____
2. LOSE SUITCASE WHO?   'Who lost a suitcase?'
   _____ whq_____
   AUNT LOSE WHAT?   'What did my aunt lose?'
   _____ whq _____
   AUNT LOSE SUITCASE WHEN?   'When did my aunt lose her suitcase?'
   _____ whq_____
   AUNT LOSE SUITCASE WHICH?   'Which suitcase did my aunt lose?'
   _____ whq _____
3. NOW VISIT S-D WHO?   'Who is visiting San Diego now?'
   _____ whq _____
   WIFE NOW VISIT WHERE?   'Where is your wife visiting now?'
   _____ whq _____
   WIFE NOW VISIT S-D WHAT-FOR?   'Why is your wife now visiting San Diego?'
   _____whq_____
   WIFE NOW VISIT S-D WHY?   'Why is your wife now visiting San Diego?'
   _____ whq _____
4. HORSE ESCAPE HOW?   'How did the horse escape?'
   _____ whq_____
   HORSE ESCAPE WHEN?   'When did the horse escape?'
   _____whq _____
   HORSE ESCAPE WHICH?   'Which horse escaped?'

_____ whq _____
5. T-V BREAK WHEN? 'When did the TV break?'
_____ whq _____
BREAK LONG-AGO WHAT? 'What broke a long time ago?'
_____ whq _____
T-V BREAK HOW? 'How did the TV break?'

EXERCISE 8.2

_____ whq _____
1. WHAT ARRIVE YESTERDAY? 'What arrived yesterday?'
_____ whq _____
WHAT ARRIVE YESTERDAY WHAT? 'What arrived yesterday?'
_____ whq _____
WHEN T-T-Y ARRIVE? 'When did the TTY arrive?'
_____ whq _____
WHEN T-T-Y ARRIVE WHEN? 'When did the TTY arrive?'
_____ whq _____
2. WHO LOSE SUITCASE? 'Who lost a suitcase?'
_____ whq _____
WHO LOSE SUITCASE WHO? 'Who lost a suitcase?'
_____ whq _____
WHAT AUNT LOSE? 'What did my aunt lose?'
_____ whq _____
WHAT AUNT LOSE WHAT? 'What did my aunt lose?'
_____ whq _____
WHEN AUNT LOSE SUITCASE? 'When did my aunt lose her suitcase?'
_____ whq _____
WHEN AUNT LOSE SUITCASE WHEN? 'When did my aunt lose her suitcase?'
_____ whq _____
WHICH SUITCASE AUNT LOSE? 'Which suitcase did my aunt lose?'
_____ whq _____
WHICH SUITCASE AUNT LOSE WHICH? 'Which suitcase did my aunt lose?'
_____ whq _____
3. WHO NOW VISIT S-D? 'Who is visiting San Diego now?'
_____ whq _____
WHO NOW VISIT S-D WHO? 'Who is visiting San Diego now?'
_____ whq _____
WHERE WIFE NOW VISIT? 'Where is your wife visiting now?'
_____ whq _____
WHERE WIFE NOW VISIT WHERE? 'Where is your wife visiting now?'
_____ whq _____
WHAT-FOR WIFE NOW VISIT S-D? 'Why is your wife now visiting San Diego?'
_____ whq _____
WHAT-FOR WIFE NOW VISIT S-D WHAT-FOR? 'Why is your wife now visiting San Diego?'
_____ whq _____
WHY WIFE NOW VISIT S-D? 'Why is your wife now visiting San Diego?'
_____ whq _____
WHY WIFE NOW VISIT S-D WHY? 'Why is your wife now visiting San Diego?'
_____ whq _____
4. HOW HORSE ESCAPE? 'How did the horse escape?'
_____ whq _____
HOW HORSE ESCAPE HOW? 'How did the horse escape?'
_____ whq _____   _____
WHEN HORSE ESCAPE? 'When did the horse escape?'
_____ whq _____
WHEN HORSE ESCAPE WHEN? 'When did the horse escape?'

260

_____ whq _____
WHICH HORSE ESCAPE? 'Which horse escaped?'
_____ whq _____
WHICH HORSE ESCAPE WHICH? 'Which horse escaped?'
_____ whq _____

5. _____ whq _____
WHEN T-V BREAK? 'When did the TV break?'
_____ whq _____
WHEN T-V BREAK WHEN? 'When did the TV break?'
_____ whq _____
WHAT BREAK LONG-AGO? 'What broke a long time ago?'
_____ whq _____
WHAT BREAK LONG-AGO WHAT? 'What broke a long time ago?'
____ whq _____
HOW T-V BREAK? 'How did the TV break?'
_____ whq _____
HOW T-V BREAK HOW? 'How did the TV break?'

EXERCISE 8.3

_____ y _____
1. YES, SHE DRAW HERSELF. 'Yes, she drew it herself.'
_____ y _____
2. YES, I I-TELL-HIM MYSELF. 'Yes, I'll tell him myself.'
_____ y _____
3. YES, I CLEAN-UP MYSELF. 'Yes, I cleaned it up myself.'
_____ y _____
4. YES, THEY DECIDE WRITE THEMSELVES. 'Yes, they decided to write it themselves.'
_____ y _____
5. YES, HE WRITE HIMSELF. 'Yes, he wrote it himself.'
_____ y _____
6. YES, HE BUILD HIMSELF. 'Yes, he built it himself.'
_____ y _____
7. YES, I GROW MYSELF. 'Yes, I grew them myself.'
_____ y ____
8. YES, HE WASH HIMSELF. 'Yes, he washed it himself.'

EXERCISE 8.4

_____ t ___ _____ n _____
1. TYPEWRITER MYSELF NOT HAVE. 'I don't have a typewriter.'
2. HIMSELF LONELY HE. 'He's lonely.'
3. HERSELF HAVE SKILL. 'She has the ability.'
_____ n _____
4. THEMSELVES ENTHUSIASTIC STUDY NOT. 'They're not eager to study.'
_____ q _____
5. TEST YOURSELF WORRY YOU? 'Are you worried about the test?'
_____ q _____
6. ANY QUESTION YOURSELF HAVE? 'Do you have any questions?'

EXERCISE 9.1

_____ y _____
1. COP SHE-GIVE-HIM TICKET. 'The cop gave him a ticket.'
_____ y _____
2. YES, TOMORROW TIME 3 HAVE MEETING. 'Yes, there's a meeting at 3 o'clock tomorrow.'

_____ y _____
3. YES, I HAVE NEW BICYCLE.   'Yes, I have a new bicycle.'
_____ n _____
4. NO, I NEED GAS.   'No, I need gas.'
_____ y _____
5. I HAVE HEARING-AID.   'Yes, I have a hearing aid.'
_____ n _____
6. NOT TO-TELEPHONE, TELEPHONE BREAK.   'Don't call, the telephone is broken.'
_____ y _____
7. YES, I HAVE TYPEWRITER.   'Yes, I have a typewriter.'
_____ n _____
8. I NOT HAVE KEY.   'I don't have the key.'
_____ n _____
9. i NOT HAVE BOOK.   'I don't have a book.'
10. I WANT AIRPLANE.   'I want (to use) an airplane.'

EXERCISE 9.2

__ t _____
1. GIRLFRIEND HAVE BLOND HAIR.   'My girlfriend, she has blond hair.'
___ t _____
2. CALIFORNIA WOW NICE.   'California, it's very nice.'
___ t ___
3. TEACHER SHE-BAWL-OUT-HIM.   'The teacher, she bawled him out.'
__ t _
4. RAIN STOP.   'The rain, it stopped.'
___ t __
5. LEADER SHE-ASK-ME QUESTION.   'The leader, she asked me a question.'
_____ t _____
6. HIS WRIST-WATCH STEAL.   'His wrist watch, it was stolen.'
__ t _ _____ n _____
7. TREE IT NOT LOOK GOOD.   'The tree, it doesn't look good.'
____ t _____
8. PERFORMANCE WONDERFUL.   'The performance, it was wonderful.'
__ t __
9. PLANT NEED WATER.   'The plant, it needs water.'
___ t ___
10. MEETING CANCEL.   'The meeting, it was cancelled.'

EXERCISE 10.1

1. SHE SEE DOCTOR SHOULD SHE.   'She should see a doctor.'
_____ q _____
2. LETTER YOU GET WILL YOU?   'Will you get a letter?'
3. TOMORROW PRESIDENT APPEAR MAYBE.   'The president may show up tomorrow.'
4. HE RECOVER WILL HE.   'He'll get well.'
5. I WIN RACE MUST I.   'I must win the race.'
6. I LIPREAD CAN.   'I can lipread.'
7. LETTER I TYPE 1-MINUTE CAN I.   'I can type a letter in a minute.'
8. S-F YOU VISIT MUST YOU.   'You must visit San Francisco.'
9. HE TAKE-UP MORE CLASS SHOULD HE.   'He should take more classes.'
10. SISTER MARRY WILL.   'My sister will get married.'

EXERCISE 10.2

1. SHE SHOULD SEE DOCTOR SHE.   'She should see a doctor.'
_____ q _____
2. LETTER YOU WILL GET YOU?   'Will you get a letter?'

262

3. TOMORROW PRESIDENT MAYBE APPEAR.   'The president may show up tomorrow.'
4. HE WILL RECOVER HE.   'He'll get well.'
5. I MUST WIN RACE I.   'I must win the race.'
6. I CAN LIPREAD.   'I can lipread.'
7. LETTER I CAN TYPE 1-MINUTE I.   'I can type a letter in a minute.'
8. S-F YOU MUST VISIT YOU.   'You must visit San Francisco.'
9. HE SHOULD TAKE-UP MORE CLASS HE.   'He should take more classes.'
10. SISTER WILL MARRY.   'My sister will get married.'

EXERCISE 10.3

_____ n _____
1. I STAY 1-HOUR CAN'T I.   'I can't stay an hour.'

_____ n _____
2. HE ACCEPT RESPONSIBILITY REFUSE HE.   'He won't take responsibility.'

_____ n _____
3. HE NOT-YET COOK FOOD HE.   'He hasn't cooked the food.'

_____ n _____
4. I GET-UP TIME 6 CAN'T I.   'I can't get up at six.'

_____ n _____
5. TELEPHONE NUMBER HE MEMORIZE NOT-YET HE.   'He hasn't memorized the telephone
number.'

_____ n _____
6. SHE BORN BABY NOT-YET SHE.   'She hasn't had her baby yet.'

_____ n _____
7. MAN HE HE-PAY-ME REFUSE HE.   'The man refuses to pay me.'

_____ n _____
8. LETTER HE-SEND-ME NOT-YET HE.   'He hasn't sent me a letter.'

_____ n _____
9. I NOT-YET TRY ESTABLISH C-L-U-B I.   'I haven't tried setting up a club.'

_____ n _____
10. ADDRESS SHE PUT-DOWN FOR-YOU CAN'T SHE.   'She can't write down the address for you.'

EXERCISE 10.4

_____ n ___
1. NO, I CAN'T I.   'No, I can't.'

_____ y _____
2. YES, SHE SHOULD.   'Yes, she should.'

_____ y _____
3. YES, I MAYBE I.   'Yes, I may.'

_____ y _____
4. YES, YOU CAN.   'Yes, you can.'

_____ n _____
5. NO, HE NOT-YET HE.   'No, he hasn't.'

_____ y ____
6. YES, SHE FINISH.   'Yes, she did.'

_____ y _____
7. YES, YOU SHOULD.   'Yes, you should.'

_____ y _____
8. YES, HE MAYBE HE.   'Yes, he may.'

_____ y ____
9. YES, SHE WILL SHE.   'Yes, she will.'

263

DIALOGUE 3

Jack: I just saw an interesting movie. It's an old movie, a sign presentation by George Veditz. Have you seen it?
Tom: No, I haven't. Who is this Veditz?
Jack: He was deaf, and was president of the N.A.D. back in 1913. You can see that his signs are older and different.
Tom: Why was the movie made?
Jack: The N.A.D. raised 5,000 dollars to make movies. They wanted to preserve and protect sign language for future generations of deaf people.
Tom: I'd like to see the movie. Where is it?
Jack: The library should have it. Ask your library.

EXERCISE 11.1

1. MY HOME HERE.   'My home is here.'
   MY HOME THERE.   'My home is over there.'
2. .YOUR GLASSES HERE.   'Your glasses are here.'
   YOUR GLASSES THERE.   'Your glasses are over there.'
3. CAR HERE.   'The car is here.'
   CAR THERE.   'The car is over there.'
4. COKE MACHINE HERE.   'The coke machine is here.'
   COKE MACHINE THERE.   'The coke machine is over there.' ˙
5. WOMAN HERE.   'The woman is here.'
   WOMAN THERE.   'The woman is over there.'
6. STORE HERE.   'The store is here.'
   STORE THERE.   'The store is over there.'
7. BASEBALL GAME HERE.   'The baseball game is here.'
   BASEBALL GAME THERE.   'The baseball game is over there.'
8. CHURCH OLD HERE.   'The old church is here.'
   CHURCH OLD THERE.   'The old church is over there.'
9. PAPER HERE.   'The paper is here.'
   PAPER THERE.   'The paper is over there.'
10. YOUR FRIEND HERE.   'Your friend is here.'
    YOUR FRIEND THERE.   'Your friend is over there.'

EXERCISE 11.2

1. BEFORE I WALK-THERE I.   'I walked there before.'
2. BEFORE I FLY-THERE I.   'I flew there before.'
3. FURNITURE HEAVY SHE MOVE-THERE.   'She moved the heavy furniture there.'
4. BEFORE YOU DRIVE-HERE YOU.   'You drove here before.'
5. BEFORE YOU WALK-HERE YOU.   'You walked here before.'
6. BEFORE YOU FLY-HERE YOU.   'You flew here before.'
7. BOOK MANY SHE PUT-HERE.   'She put many books here.'
8. CHICAGO, L-A HE THERE-DRIVE-THERE HE.   'He drove from Chicago to Los Angeles.'
9. CHICAGO, L-A HE THERE-FLY-THERE HE.   'He flew from Chicago to Los Angeles.'
10. STORE, YOUR HOME SHE THERE-DRIVE-THERE.   'She drove from the store to your home.'
11. STORE, YOUR HOME SHE THERE-BRING-THERE.   'She brought it from the store to your home.'

EXERCISE 11.3

1. CHICAGO HE MOVE-THERE, STAY 2 YEAR FINISH
   HE THERE-MOVE-THERE WASHINGTON.   'He moved to Chicago, stayed there for two years then he moved from there to Washington.'

2. C-F NOW I GIVE-YOU FINISH
   YOU-GIVE-HIM TOMORROW.   'I'll give you the captioned film now then you can give it to him tomorrow.'
3. I STAY-HERE 1-WEEK WITH SISTER FINISH
   I GO-THERE VISIT MOTHER.   'I'm staying here for a week with my sister, then I'll go and visit my mother.'
4. BREAKFAST I COOK FINISH YOU
   WASH-DISH.   'I'll cook breakfast, then you can wash the dishes.'
5. SUITCASE I PACK FINISH I GO-THERE AIRPORT.   'I'll pack my suitcase then I'm going to the airport.'
6. PERFORMANCE PRACTICE ALL-DAY FINISH
   TONIGHT HAVE PARTY THERE MY HOME.   'We'll practice our play all day then tonight there'll be a party at my home.'

EXERCISE 12.1

1. IT RESTAURANT HAVE FOOD.   'There's food at the restaurant.'
2. IT HOME HAVE TEA.   'There's tea at home.'
3. IT STORE HAVE SHOES.   'There are shoes at that store.'
4. IT SCHOOL HAVE DEAF STUDENT.   'There are deaf students at that school.'
5. IT RESTAURANT HAVE MEAT.   'There's meat at that restaurant.'
6. IT KITCHEN HAVE TABLE.   'There's a table in that kitchen.'
7. IT HOUSE HAVE CHAIR.   'There's a chair in the house.'
8. IT RESTAURANT HAVE RESTROOM.   'There's a restroom in the restaurant.'
9. IT R-E-F HAVE CREAM.   'There's cream in the refrigerator.'
10. IT BOOK HAVE SIGN.   'There are (pictures of) signs in the book.'

EXERCISE 12.2

1. WOMAN CL:∧-THERE, SHE-LOOK-AT-ME.   'The woman stood over there and looked at me.'
2. I ENTER, LETTER CL:B-THERE.   'I went in, and the letter was lying there.'
3. SHOULD BICYCLE CL:3-THERE.   'The bicycle should be parked there.'
4. SURPRISED ME. PRESIDENT CL:∧-HERE.   'I was surprised! The President was standing right next to me.'

          _____ t _____
5. CAR BLUE CL:3-THERE, THAT-ONE HIS.   'The blue car parked over there, that's his.'
6. SHE FORGET LEAVE MAGAZINE CL:B-THERE.   'She forgot and left the magazine lying there.'
7. RECENTLY BROTHER CL:∧-HERE, NOW GONE.   'My brother was just standing right here, and now he's gone.'
8. CAR CL:3-THERE, NOW PUT-IN-GAS.   'The car is standing over there and now they're putting in some gas.'

EXERCISE 12.3

1. I SEE BEER CL:C-ON-TOP-OF-CL:B.   'I saw a beer can on top of the table.'
2. I SEE CAR CL:3-UNDER-CL:B.   'I saw a car parked in the garage.'
3. I SEE PAPER CL:B-NEXT-TO-CL:B.   'I saw two sheets of paper next to each other.'
4. I SEE PEOPLE CL:∧-BEHIND-CL:∧.   'I saw two people standing in line.'
5. I SEE PLANT CL:C-AND-CL:C-ON-TOP-OF-CL:B.   'I saw two small potted plants on a shelf.'
6. I SEE CL:F-NEXT-TO-CL:F.   'I saw two bottle tops next to each other.'
7. I SEE WOMAN CL:∧-UNDER-CL:B.   'I saw a woman under an awning.'

EXERCISE 13.1

1. HE CRAZY-FOR CHEESE, HAVE PLENTY I.   'He really likes cheese and I've got plenty.'

                                        ___t___
2. SPORTS RESIDENTIAL-SCHOOL HAVE SOME.   'The school for the deaf has some sports.'
                              ___t___
3. WATER CALIFORNIA NOW HAVE PLENTY.   'California now has plenty of water.'
                        ___t_
4. MEAT IT HAVE LEFT IT A-LITTLE.   'There is a little meat left.'
                ___t___
5. YOUR PIE GRANDMOTHER WANT SOME.   'Grandmother wants some of your pie.'

EXERCISE 13.2

1. DOG IT WANT CL:L̈ WATER.   'The dog wants a lot of water.'
2. MY HOUSE WOW DIRTY. HAVE CL:G D-U-S-T.   'My house is very dirty with a lot of dust.'
3. BASEMENT, I FIND CL:BB↑↓WATER.   'I found a lot of water in the basement!'
4. YESTERDAY, CL:BB↑↓ PAPER I THROW-AWAY.   'I threw away a pile of papers yesterday.'
5. CL:L̈ O-J YOU DRINK SHOULD YOU.   'You should drink a lot of orange juice.'
6. RECENTLY HE-GIVE-ME CL:BB↑↓ LETTER.   'He gave me a stack of letters recently.'
7. RAIN STOP FINISH, LEFT M-U-D CL:L̈.   'The rain left a lot of mud when it stopped.'

EXERCISE 13.3

1. STORE IT HAVE CL:5̈5̈ BICYCLE.   'The store has a large number of bicycles.'
2. H-O-T-E-L IT HAVE DOOR++.   'The hotel has many doors.'
3. MY SISTER FINISH HAVE CL:5̈5̈ BOYFRIEND.   'My sister already has a large number of boy-
                                                                    friends.'
4. I LIKE HOUSE WITH WINDOW++.   'I like houses with many windows.'
5. THERE PARTY I SEE CL:5̈5̈ CHILDREN.   'I saw a large number of children at the party.'
6. I MUST WRITE LIST++.   'I must write many lists.'
7. HE HAVE BEAUTIFUL GLASS++.   'He has many beautiful glasses.'

EXERCISE 13.4

       ___t___
1. BIRTHDAY HE-GIVE-ME 7-DOLLAR.   'He gave me 7 dollars for my birthday.'
2. I FIND 50-CENT YESTERDAY I.   'I found 50 cents yesterday.'
3. I WIN 300 DOLLAR I.   'I won 300 dollars.'
4. LONG-AGO T-T-Y COST 40 DOLLAR.   'A long time ago TTY's cost 40 dollars.'
5. LONG-AGO I BUY PENCIL COST 4-CENT.   'I used to buy pencils for 4 cents.'
       ___t_____
6. MY CAR OLD SELL 450 DOLLAR.   'I sold my old car for 450 dollars.'
       _____q_____
7. 20-DOLLAR YOU NEED TODAY?   'Do you need the 20 dollars today?'

DIALOGUE 4

Bill: Did you know there's a new play? A Deaf theatre group has been established in Los Angeles. Do
        you want to see it?
Jack: Yes, I would like to. Are there any seats left?
Bill: There should be a lot left. I will call them and reserve seats for the two of us. The tickets cost 3
        dollars each.
Jack: I can pay you now. Do you want to drive up there together?
Bill: Fine. We can watch the play then go to a friend's house for a party, talk with some friends then
        come on home.
Jack: What time should I meet you tomorrow?
Bill: At four o'clock. We will have plenty of time to drive up there.

EXERCISE 14.1

_____ n _____
1. I NONE HEAR YOU MARRY YOU. 'I didn't hear you got married.'
_____ n _____
I HEAR ~NONE YOU MARRY YOU. 'I didn't hear you got married.'

_____ t _____ _____ n _____
2. NURSE GIVE-SHOT, I NONE FEEL I. 'I felt nothing when the nurse gave me a shot.'
_____ t _____ ____ n _____
NURSE GIVE-SHOT, I FEEL ~NONE I. 'I felt nothing when the nurse gave me a shot.'

___ t ___ _____ n _____
3. WRENCH STORE IT NONE HAVE. 'The store doesn't have a wrench.'
___ t ___ _____ n _____
WRENCH STORE IT HAVE ~NONE. The store doesn't have a wrench.'

_____ n _____
4. IT C-O NONE HAVE DEAF WORK. 'The company doesn't have any Deaf workers.'
_____ n _____
IT C-O HAVE ~NONE DEAF WORK. 'The company doesn't have any Deaf workers.'

_____ n _____
5. MAN NEVER INTERACT DEAF HE. 'The man never associates with Deaf people.'
_____ n _____
MAN INTERACT DEAF NEVER HE. 'The man never associates with Deaf people.'

_t _ _____ n _____
6. C-F HE NONE GET HE. 'He didn't get the captioned film.'
_t _ _____ n _____
C-F HE GET NONE HE. 'He didn't get the captioned film.'

___ t _ _ n _____
7. TURKEY I NONE EAT. 'I didn't eat any turkey.'
__ t ___ _ n _____
TURKEY I EAT ~NONE. 'I didn't eat any turkey.'

_____ t _____ ___ n _____
8. MONEY YOU-GIVE-HER, I NONE SEE I. 'I didn't see the money you gave her.'
_____ t _____ ___ n _____
MONEY YOU-GIVE-HER, I SEE ~NONE I. 'I didn't see the money you gave her.'

_____ t _____ _____ n _____
9. WOMAN SHE NEVER SHE-HELP-ME SHE. 'The woman never helped me.'
_____ t _____ _____ n _____
WOMAN SHE SHE-HELP-ME NEVER SHE. 'The woman never helped me.'

_t _ _____ n _____
10. T-V I NONE UNDERSTAND I. 'I can't understand the television at all.'
_t _ _____ n _____
T-V I UNDERSTAND ~NONE I. 'I can't understand the television at all.'

_____ n _____
11. HE NEVER BATHE HE. 'He never bathes.'
_____ n _____
HE BATHE NEVER HE. 'He never bathes.'

EXERCISE 14.2

_____ n _____
1. SHE BUY NOTHING. ''She bought nothing.'
_____ n _____
2. NOW YEAR, I GROW NOTHING. 'I didn't grow anything this year.'
_____ t _____ _____ n _____
3. NURSE GIVE-SHOT, I FEEL NOTHING I. 'I felt nothing when the nurse gave me a shot.'

267

_____ n _____
4. NONE PEOPLE RIDE B-U-S. 'No one rides the bus.'

_ t _____ n _____
5. Z-O-O IT HAVE NONE MONKEY. 'There are no monkeys at the zoo.'

_____ n _____
6. I MUST SHOP, HAVE NONE FOOD LEFT. 'I have no food left so I must shop.'

____ t ___ _____ n _____
7. WORK P-O, HE EARN NOTHING. 'He makes nothing working at the post office.'

_____ n _____
8. REALLY I-INFORM-YOU, HAVE NONE TIME I. 'Really I must tell you I have no time.'

_____ n _____
9. YESTERDAY FRIEND HE LEARN NONE SIGN. 'My friend didn't learn any signs yesterday.'

_ t _____ n _____
10. A-A-A-D, I DO-WORK NOTHING. 'I didn't do anything for the American Athletic Association of the Deaf.'

EXERCISE 14.3

_____ t _____ ____ n _____
1. LETTER SHE-SEND-HIM, NOTHING SHE. 'She didn't send him the letter.'

_____ t _____ ____ n ___
2. SHIRT NEW WASH-IN-MACHINE, NOTHING I. 'I didn't wash the new shirt in the machine.

_____ t _____ ____ n ___
3. I RESPONSIBLE CAR-ACCIDENT, NOTHING I. 'I am not responsible for the car accident.'

_____ t _____ ____ n ___
4. I I-TTY-YOU YESTERDAY NIGHT, NOTHING I. 'I didn't call you on the TTY last night.'

_____ t _____ ____ n ___
5. I I-WARN-HIM FINISH, NOTHING I. 'I didn't warn him.'

____ t _____ ____ n ___
6. I-BOTHER-HIM, NOTHING I. 'I wasn't bothering him.'

_____ t _____ ____ n _____
7. BOY STEAL CAMERA, NOTHING HE. 'The boy didn't steal the camera.'

EXERCISE 15.1

_____ q _____
1. DON'T-MIND I-BORROW-HER DICTIONARY? 'Do you mind if I borrow her dictionary?'

_____ n _____
2. I UNDERSTAND. I DON'T-WANT I-TAKE-ADVANTAGE-HIM. 'I understand. I don't want to take advantage of him.'

_ t __
3. READY, I HAPPY I-SUMMON-HER. 'When it's ready I'll be happy to call her.'

_____ t _____
4. HIS SCHEDULE I-COPY-HIM CAN I. 'I can copy his schedule.'

5. I WANT I-CHOOSE-HER. 'I would like to choose her.'

EXERCISE 15.2

_____ t _____
1. HER HOMEWORK YOU-COPY-HER. 'You copied her homework.'

_____ q _____
2. CAN YOU-TAKE-HIM THERE Z-O-O? 'Can you take him to the zoo?'

____ t _____
3. YOU READY LEAVE, YOU-SUMMON-HIM. 'Now that you're ready to go, go get him.'

4. NOT LIKE YOU-TAKE-ADVANTAGE-HER. 'I don't like your taking advantage of her.'
5. SURPRISE YOU-CHOOSE-HIM PRESIDENT C-L-U-B. 'I'm surprised you elected him as president of the club.'

EXERCISE 15.3

YESTERDAY I I-TELL-THEM-TWO, RAIN WILL. 'I told the two of them that it would rain.'
   — t —
2. MONEY HE-GIVE-TWO-THEM. 'He gave the two of them some money.'
3. BETTER YOU-ASK-TWO-THEM. SURE YOU RIGHT YOU. 'You had better ask the two of them. Be sure you are right.'
4. I WANT I-TAKE-YOU-TWO THERE RESTAURANT. 'I want to take both of you to the restaurant.'
5. YOU-PL. BEST, I WANT I-CHOOSE-YOU-TWO. 'You are the best, I want to pick both of you.'
6. BEER I-CL:C-GIVE-TWO-THEM. 'I gave the two of them some beer.'
   _____ t ____
7. DAUGHTER I I-SEND-TWO-THEM LETTER WILL I. 'I'll send my two daughters a letter.'

EXERCISE 15.4

   — t —
1. THIEF COP FINISH HE-CATCH-EACH-OF-THEM. 'The cop caught each of the thiefs.'
   _____ q _____ .
2. PLEASE FOR ME, CAN YOU YOU-ASK-ALL-OF-THEM? 'Could you please ask all of them for me?'
3. WANT I I-INVITE-EACH-OF-THEM MY WEDDING. 'I would like to invite each of them to my wedding.'
4. TOMORROW I I-INFORM-ALL-OF-YOU WHO WIN. 'I'll let you all know who won tomorrow.'
   ____ t _____
5. MY OLD CLOTHES WILL I I-GIVE-ALL-OF-THEM. 'I'll give my old clothes to all of them.
6. FINISH I I-TELL-ALL-OF-YOU MUST YOU-PL. COME-HERE TIME 8. 'I already told all of you that you had to come here at 8 o'clock.'
   _____ t _____
7. THEY CHILDREN MOTHER SHE-SEND-EACH-OF-THEM BOX. 'The mother sent each of the children a box.'

EXERCISE 16.1

1. MOVIE IT CONTINUE 3-HOUR. 'The movie lasted for three hours.'
   _____ t _____
2. COURSE I TAKE-UP 8-WEEK. 'The course I'm taking is 8 weeks long.'
3. NOW TWO-US MARRY 7 YEAR. 'Now the two of us have been married for 7 years.'
4. FIVE-US PLAN GO-AWAY BACKPACKING MAYBE 5-DAY. 'The five of us plan to go backpacking for maybe 5 days.'
5. NOW LEFT 6-MONTH, MOVE-AWAY WILL I. 'Now there's only 6 months left then I'll be moving away.'
6. I ORDER BED NEW, I MUST WAIT 4-WEEK. 'I ordered a new bed and I have to wait 4 weeks for it.'
7. HE LOSE ALMOST 9-DAY. 'He was lost for almost 9 days.'

EXERCISE 16.2

1. F-R-A-T MEETING WILL HERE IN-FOUR-YEAR. 'There'll be a National Fraternal Society of the Deaf meeting here in 4 years.'

2. LAST TIME I I-SEE-YOU LAST-YEAR, RIGHT?   'The last time I saw you was last year, right?'
3. 25 YEAR PAST HARD FIND INTERPRETER.   '25 years ago it was hard to find an interpreter.'
4. PARTY THERE MY HOME IN-THREE-MONTH.   'There'll be a party at my home in three months.'
5. I GO-THERE FINISH SIX-WEEK-AGO.   'I went there six weeks ago.'
6. HE GRADUATE GALLAUDET FOUR-YEAR-AGO.   'He graduated from Gallaudet four years ago.'
7. C-O SAY WILL BRING-HERE BED IN-FOUR-WEEK.   'The company said it would bring the bed in four weeks.'

EXERCISE 16.3

1. IT-SEND-ME NEWSPAPER MONTHLY.   'They send me a newspaper every month.'
2. MUST I TAKE-PILL DAILY.   'I must take a pill everyday.'
3. SHE GO-THERE EUROPE BUSINESS MONTHLY.   'She goes to Europe on business every month.'
4. SHE EXERCISE WEEKLY.   'She exercises every week.'
5. HE TO-TELEPHONE I DAILY, I BORED I.   'He calls me every day and I'm bored.'

DIALOGUE 5

Jane: I haven't seen you for awhile. I hear you have a new job. How is it?
Ron: It's fine. I'm the only Deaf person there. They don't know sign language. I decided to set up a sign language class. It's two hours on Tuesdays.
Jane: That was a good idea. Does your boss sign and fingerspell?
Ron: A little bit. I have three bosses. I gave each of them a sign language book. They have learned a little. I should get a TTY next week. Then you can call me.
Jane: Great. Now we have six Deaf people working at my company. Will your company hire more Deaf people?
Ron: Probably.
Bill: Ready? The movie is starting now.

EXERCISE 17.1

```
_____t _____ _____n _____
```
1. FINISH ADVERTISE TOURNAMENT, I DON'T-KNOW I.   'I don't know if they have advertised the tournament.'
```
_____t _____ _____n _____
```
2. HE APPLY FOR PRESIDENT, HE DOUBT HE.   'He doubts he will apply for president.'
```
_____t _____
```
3. TWO-THEM ARGUE ALL-DAY, TEND TWO-THEM.   'They tend to argue all day.'
```
_____t _____ _____ y_____
```
4. I SUPPORT WHEELCHAIR, HE KNOW-THAT HE.   'He knows that I support the disabled.'
```
_____t _____ _____n _____
```
5. BORROW MONEY FROM BOSS, SHE DON'T-WANT SHE.   'She doesn't want to borrow money from her boss.'
```
_____t _____ ____n _____
```
6. I AGAIN BROKE, I DON'T-WANT.   'I don't want to be broke again.'
```
_____t _____
```
7. GO-BY-BOAT THERE EUROPE, THREE-US WANT.   'The three of us want to go to Europe by boat.'
```
___t ___ __n __
```
8. HE FIRED, NOT HE.   'He's not fired.'
```
_____t _____ ____y ____
```
9. HE GRANDFATHER TELL-STORY, HE LIKE HE.   'Grandfather likes to tell stories.'
```
_____t _____ ____n _____
```
10. STAY PARTY ALL-NIGHT, I DON'T-LIKE I.   'I don't like to stay at parties all night.'

EXERCISE 17.2

              _____ t _____
1. HOUSE R-E-N-T, A-P-T R-E-N-T, IT WORSE IT.   'House rent is worse (higher) than apartment rent.'

              _____ t _____
2. IT WOOD TABLE, IT METAL TABLE, I WANT IT.   'I want the wood table not the metal table.'

              _____ t _____
3. STAY HOME WATCH T-V, GO-AWAY MOVIE PAY

     _____
     5-DOLLAR, IT BETTER IT.   'It is better to stay home and watch TV than to pay five dollars to see a movie.'

              _____ t _____
4. IT FLOWER REAL, IT FLOWER S-I-L-K, IT PRETTIER IT.   'The real flower is prettier than the silk one.'

              _____ t _____ ____q____
5. IT EXPENSIVE, IT CHEAP, YOU WANT IT?   'Do you want the expensive one or the cheap one?'

              _____ t _____
6. I GO-THERE COLLEGE, I STAY WORK, I STAY I.   'I decided to stay and work rather than go to college.'

              _____ t _____
7. MEETING HERE, MEETING THERE, I PREFER IT.   'I prefer to meet here not there.'

EXERCISE 17.3

1. SHE RESEARCH A-S-L, HIT FIND RULE++.   'She was doing research on ASL, and it turned out that she found many rules.'
2. SHE GO-THERE BUY T-T-Y, HAPPEN S-A-L-E.   'She went to buy a TTY and it happened that there was a sale on them.'
3. BABY SEEM SICK, FIND HAVE EAR-ACHE.   'The baby seemed to be sick and then we found out that she had an ear ache.'
4. CLOTHES PUT-IN WASH-IN-MACHINE, FRUSTRATE RUIN.   'I put my clothes in the washing machine and to my dismay, they were ruined.'
5. I BUY GLASS NEW, WRONG DAMAGE.   'I had just bought a new glass when it was damaged.'
6. TWO-US CHAT, FIND SAME HAVE DEAF PARENTS.   'We were talking and then we found out that we both have deaf parents.'
7. I WATCH T-V, WRONG CAPTION.   'I was watching television when suddenly captions appeared (on the screen).'
8. I DRIVE-THERE, FRUSTRATE SHE NOT HOME.   'I drove there only to find her not at home.'
9. HE HAVE NEW CAR, FRUSTRATE STEAL.   'He had a new car then to his dismay, it was stolen.'
10. HE ACT NOTHING-TO-IT, WRONG SHOT-UP FAMOUS.   'He was performing in bit roles when all of a sudden, he hit it big and became famous.'

EXERCISE 18.1

1. YESTERDAY NIGHT I-TTY-YOU-REPEATEDLY (with effort), YOU NONE YOU.   'Last night I called you on the teletypewriter many times but you weren't there.'

              _____ t _____
2. PITY-HIM, TEAM HIS LOUSY, HE LOSE-COMPETITION-REPEATEDLY (carelessly).   'I feel sorry for him—his team is so bad and they always lose so badly.'

3. BROTHER TEND ANALYZE-REPEATEDLY (with attention) MOVIE.   'My brother has a tendency to analyze a movie thoroughly.'

271

4. SHE BOTHER-HIM-REPEATEDLY (carelessly),
WRONG HE-BAWL-OUT-HER. 'She kept bothering him heedlessly and then suddenly he bawled
her out.'
        __t__
5. HE THIRSTY. WATER HE DRINK-REPEATEDLY (with effort).
'He was thirsty so he kept gulping down water.'
6. SHE LOVE READ-REPEATEDLY (with ease). 'She loves to just read and read.'
      _____t_____
7. BASKETBALL, NEW-YORK BEFORE
WIN-REPEATEDLY (with ease). 'New York used to win all their basketball games easily.'
8. FINISH I-WARN-YOU REPEATEDLY (with effort)
SHOULD FIX T-I-R-E. 'I have warned you many times that you should fix that tire.'
9. BORED I-PRESENT-YOU-REPEATEDLY (with effort)
MONEY. I'm tired of having to give you money all the time.'
10. FIND HE INFORM-HIM-REPEATEDLY (with attention
POLICE. 'It was discovered that he had been diligently informing the police.'

EXERCISE 18.2

1. HE STAY-THERE-CONTINUALLY (with ease)
3-HOUR FINISH COME-HERE. 'He lingered there for 3 hours then came back.'
2. HE APPEAR NONE, I WAIT-CONTINUALLY (with effort)
'He didn't show up so I waited a long time.'
3. TRAVEL-AROUND, I WANT-CONTINUALLY (with effort).
'I've always longed to travel.'
4. SHE EAT-CONTINUALLY (carelessly),
WRONG BECOME-FAT. 'She kept eating carelessly and without realizing it she became fat.'
5. HARD UNDERSTAND HE FINGERSPELL-
CONTINUALLY (with attenton). 'It's hard to understand him because he diligently fingerspells all
the time.'
6. WOOD BURN-CONTINUALLY (with ease)
3-HOUR. 'The wood burned steadily for 3 hours.'
7. HOMEWORK I STRUGGLE-CONTINUALLY (with effort),
FINALLY I UNDERSTAND. 'I struggled mightily with my homework and finally I understood it.'

EXERCISE 19.1

1. K-A-N-S-A-S VERY-CL:BB. 'Kansas is very flat.'
2. WINTER THERE M-I-N-N VERY-COLD. 'The winters are very cold in Minnesota.'
3. HER HOME WOW VERY-SMALL. 'Her home is very small.'
4. SNOW ALL-OVER WOW VERY-WHITE. 'The snow covering everything was very white.'
5. YOUR LECTURE VERY-CLEAR. 'Your lecture was very clear.'
          _____n_____
6. YOU WORK NOTHING, VERY-LAZY YOU. 'You haven't done a thing, you're so lazy.'
7. BASKETBALL PLAYER HE WOW VERY-TALL. 'The basketball player is very tall.'
8. GAS NOW VERY-EXPENSIVE. 'Gas is now very expensive.'
9. MUST YOU GO-THERE MEETING,
IT VERY-IMPORTANT. 'You must go to the meeting, it is very important.'
    ____t____
10. RAIN SINCE, WOW VERY-WORSE. 'The rain we've been having is the worst ever.'

EXERCISE 19.2

               __whq__
1. SHE MAD-REPEATEDLY. WRONG? 'What's wrong with her? She's mad all the time.'
2. FOOTBALL PLAYER HE HURT-REPEATEDLY. 'The football player keeps getting hurt.'

3. FATHER WORRY. I LATE-REPEATEDLY I. 'My father worries because I'm always late.'
  _____n_____
4. SINCE DON'T-KNOW WHY,
   I SICK-REPEATEDLY. 'I don't know why but I keep getting sick.'
5. DOWNSTAIRS HAVE DOG,
   NOISE-REPEATEDLY AWFUL. 'There's a dog downstairs that keeps making terrible noises.'
  _____n_____
6. HE JUDGMENT NONE,
   HE WRONG-REPEATEDLY. 'He's always making mistakes because he has no judgment.'
7. HE LOOK-FOR WORK,
   FRUSTRATE-REPEATEDLY HE. 'He is frustrated everywhere he looks for work.'

EXERCISE 19.3

1. LIKE I OUTSIDE SIT, LOOK-AT
   PEOPLE DIFFERENT-CONTINUALLY. 'I like to sit outside and look at all the different people.'
  _____t_____
2. PARTY THERE, SHE EMBARRASSED-
   CONTINUALLY ALL-NIGHT. 'At the party she was continually embarrassed all night.'
  ____n_____
3. I DON'T KNOW, SEEM I WRONG-
   CONTINUALLY. 'I don't know, it seems like I'm wrong all the time.'
4. HE BUY NEW CAR, SINCE
   CAREFUL-CONTINUALLY HE. 'Ever since he bought a new car he's been very careful with it.'
5. AUNT SICK-CONTINUALLY.
   WRONG LOST #JOB. 'My aunt was always sick and then she lost her job.'
6. ALL-DAY GIRL MISCHIEVOUS-CONTINUALLY. 'The girl was mischievous all day.'
  _____t_____
7. CAPTION T-V HAVE DIFFERENT-CONTINUALLY. 'There are many different captioned TV
                                              shows.'

DIALOGUE 6

Don: In the past there were no teletypewriters, decoders, and interpreters like there are now. You
     young people have plenty of things.
Mary: When did you buy your first teletypewriter?
Don: Back in 1971.
Mary: How much did it cost?
Don: 60 dollars. Back then, teletypewriters were very big, now they're very small and cost 600 dollars.
Mary: Wow. It's worth having a teletypewriter.
Don: That's true. I remember once—I wanted to go and visit a friend; I had to drive to my friend's
     place. Sometimes I would drive there, and to my dismay, my friend wasn't there. I had to keep
     going back until I got ahold of my friend. I've been frustrated many times.
Mary: Now I just call up my friend on the teletypewriter and find that he's not home. I save my gas.
Don: That's true. Comparing the way things were in the past with the way they are now, it's better now.

EXERCISE 20.1

  _____if_____
1. AIRPLANE AGAIN POSTPONE, I MAD I. 'If the plane is delayed again, I'll be mad.'
  _____if_____
2. MONEY YOU-GIVE ME NOW, I BUY TICKET I. 'If you give me the money now, I can buy the
                                            ticket.'

273

_____ if _____

3. C-F I GET FINISH, I-INFORM-ALL-OF-YOU. 'If I get the captioned film, I'll let you all know.'

_____ if _____

4. YOU DRIVE-THERE, I GO-WITH WANT I. 'If you're driving there, I'd like to go with you.'

_____ if _____

5. T-V CAPTION HAVE HE, I GO-
THERE HIS HOME. 'If he has a decoder, I'll go to his home.'

_____ if _____

6. T-V HAVE ACTOR DEAF IT,
I WATCH MUST I. 'If there's a television show with a deaf actor, then I have to watch it.'

_____ if _____

7. LEARN SIGN HE WANT,
PRACTICE MUST HE. 'If he wants to learn to sign, he has to practice.'

EXERCISE 20.2

_ rq _

1. THEY FINISH VOTE PRESIDENT C-L-U-B, WHO? BROTHER. 'They've elected a president for the club and who is it?? My brother.'

___ rq _____

2. NOW RESEARCH-REPEATEDLY SIGN, WHAT-FOR? UNDERSTAND LANGUAGE. 'Now they're doing a lot of research on sign language—why? To understand language.'

_ t _   ___ rq ___

3. CAR I FINISH DECIDE BUY, WHICH? D-A-T-S-U-N. 'I've decided to buy a car—which one? A Datsun.'

___ rq _

4. HE LECTURE-REPEATEDLY, WHAT?
ABOUT C-L-E-R-C, HIMSELF DEAF. 'He frequently lectures on what? Clerc, who is deaf.'

5. I GO-THERE PUT-IN-GAS.

___ rq ___

HOW-MUCH? 20 DOLLAR. 'I went to get gas, and how much was it? 20 dollars.'

_ rq _

6. YOU GO-TO-IT CLOSE-DOOR. WHY?
BUG ENTER-REPEATEDLY. 'Go and close the door. Why? Because the bugs keep coming in.'

EXERCISE 21.1

1. WOW VERY-BIG AIRPORT,
HAVE AIRPLANE CL:ᴛᴵ-IN-A-ROW. 'Wow, it's an enormous airport; there's a whole row of airplanes.'

2. BEFORE NONE, NOW HAVE DEAF
BUSINESS CL:Å-ALL-OVER. 'Before there weren't any but now there are businesses run by Deaf people all over.'

3. I LOOK-AT, SEE BIRD CL:V̈-IN-A-ROW. 'I looked and saw some birds sitting in a row.'

4. ARMY READY, IT HAVE AIRPLANE
CL:ᴛᴵ-IN-A-ROW. 'The military is prepared; they have airplanes lined up in a row.'

5. PARTY FINISH, WOW BEER CAN
CL:C-ALL-OVER. 'After the party, there were beer cans all over the place.'

_____ t _____

6. NOW PRICE HIGH, CAR NEW CL:3-IN-A-ROW
CAN'T SELL. 'Now prices are high, they can't sell the row of new cars.'

274

7. BEER CAN FATHER ENJOY COLLECT.
   THERE HOME HAVE CL:C-IN-A-ROW.   'My father enjoys collecting beer cans. At home there's a row of cans.'

EXERCISE 21.2

<pre>   _ n _____</pre>
1. CL:1(3)-THERE-TO-THERE, I SEE ~NONE.   'I didn't see the three of them pass by.'
2. GIRL CL:1(2)-THERE-TO-HERE CHAT FINISH,
   CL:1(2)-HERE-TO-THERE.   'The two girls came up to me, talked a bit, then left.'
3. BOY CL:1(5)-THERE-TO-HERE, DEMAND MONEY.
   I SHOCK. 'Five boys came up to me and demanded my money. I was stunned.'
4. BEAR CL:1(2)-THERE-TO-HERE,
   I HERE-RUN-THERE.   'Two bears came up to me, I ran in the opposite direction.'
<pre>   _____ q _____ _____ whq _____</pre>
5. CAN CL:1(4)-HERE-TO-THERE, ASK-HIM TIME MEETING WHAT?   'Can the four of us go up to him and ask him what time the meeting is?'

EXERCISE 21.3

<pre>   _____ y _____</pre>
1. HAVE LEFT CL:B.   'There's a lot left.'
<pre>   _____ y _____</pre>
   CL:B HAVE LEFT.   'There's a lot left.'
2. I HAVE CL:BB.   'I've got a big pile.'
   CL:BB I HAVE.   'I've got a big pile.'
<pre>   ____-_ y _____</pre>
3. I HAVE CL:BB.   'I've got a big pile of them.'
<pre>   _____ y _____</pre>
   CL:BB I HAVE.   'I've got a big pile of them.'
<pre>   _____ y _____</pre>
4. I FINISH TAKE CL:B.   'I already took a lot.'
<pre>   _____ y _____</pre>
   CL:B I FINISH TAKE.   'I already took a lot.'
<pre>   _____ y _____</pre>
5. SHE HAVE CL:44.   'She has a lot of them.'
<pre>   _____ y _____</pre>
   CL:44 SHE HAVE.   'She has a lot of them.'
6. CL:44 WANT BUY TICKET.   'There's a lot of people who want to buy tickets.'
<pre>   _____ y _____</pre>
7. IT HAVE CL:BB.   'They have a big pile of them.'
<pre>   _____ y _____</pre>
   CL:BB IT HAVE.   'They have a big pile of them.'

EXERCISE 22.1

1. OUTLINE-DINNER BELL-TRIANGULAR-SHAPED.
2. OUTLINE-HEADBOARD-BED.
3. OUTLINE-SWIMMING-POOL-L-SHAPED.
4. OUTLINE-COIL-OR-SPRING.
5. OUTLINE-LEAF.
6. OUTLINE-HEARTBEAT-MONITOR.
7. OUTLINE-CLOSED-CAPTIONING-SYMBOL.

EXERCISE 22.2

1. SHAPE-ARABIAN-TENT.
2. SHAPE-ROAD-THAT-ENDS-ABRUPTLY-AT-A-DROPOFF.
3. SHAPE-WRINKLED-CARPET.
4. SHAPE-ICY-SURFACE.
5. SHAPE-STAIRS
6. SHAPE-CHINESE-WOK.
7. SHAPE-MOUNTAIN-RANGE.

EXERCISE 22.3

1. BEFORE I WORK FACTORY COKE CL:44→. 'I used to work in a coke factory on an assembly line.'

   BEFORE I WORK FACTORY CAN CL:44→. 'I used to work in a can factory on an assembly line.'

   BEFORE I WORK FACTORY FISH CL:44→. 'I used to work in a fish factory on an assembly line.'

   BEFORE I WORK FACTORY CAR CL:44→. 'I used to work in an auto factory on an assembly line.'

2. MEETING IMPORTANT DEAF CL:55↕↕ 'A lot of Deaf people came to the important meeting.'

   MEETING IMPORTANT COP CL:55↕↕. 'A lot of cops came to the important meeting.'

   MEETING IMPORTANT INTERPRETER CL:55↕↕. 'A lot of interpreters came to the important meeting.'

   MEETING IMPORTANT RESEARCHER CL:55↕↕. 'A lot of researchers came to the important meeting.'

3. #BUSY HE DAILY STUDENT CL:44→HIS ROOM. 'He is so busy, everyday students keep filing into his office.'

   #BUSY HE DAILY SICK PEOPLE CL:44→HIS ROOM. 'He is so busy, everyday sick people keep filing into his office.'

   #BUSY HE DAILY ACTOR CL:44→HIS ROOM. 'He is so busy, everyday actors keep filing into his office.'

   #BUSY HE DAILY BOY, GIRL CL:44→HIS ROOM. 'He is so busy, everyday boys and girls keep filing into his office.'

4. AWFUL ALL-NIGHT #GAS CL:4↓. 'It was awful, the gas had been leaking all night.'

   AWFUL ALL-NIGHT NOSE CL:4↓. 'It was awful, my nose had been running all night.'

   AWFUL ALL-NIGHT TOILET CL:4↓. 'It was awful, the toilet had been leaking all night.'

   AWFUL ALL-NIGHT ROOF CL:4↓. 'It was awful, the roof had been leaking all night.'

DIALOGUE 7

Jack: I got a television decoder last week. It's really wonderful.

Alice: I have ordered one. I'm still waiting; it hasn't arrived. What does it look like?

Jack: It has a flat top, is about this long, and it's made of metal. It has a channel knob. If there is a captioned show on television, you set it on "Caption" and the captions will appear.

Alice: They made some decoders but then they had a run on the market. They did not expect that. Now they are starting to produce and sell more.

Jack: Do you know how the decoder works? The television screen is made up of several horizontal lines, one of which is line 21. That one has the caption signal. You must have a box, the television decoder, which you plug in to make the captions appear.

Alice: That's really wonderful. I can't wait to get mine.

VOCABULARY INDEX

below 148
beneath 148
BEST 169
BETTER 169
BETWEEN 111
BICYCLE 72, 105
BIG 17
BIRD 180
birth 111,148
BIRTHDAY 148
bitter 199
BLACK 36
Black person 36
BLIND 237
block 209
BLOND 101
BLOOD 207
BLUE 36
BLUSH 228
BOAT 102
BODY 83
BOOK 36, 103
booklet 137
BORED 180
boring 170
BORN 111, 148
BORROW 169
BOSS 180
BOTH 83
BOTHER 159
BOTTLE 72
BOWL 237
BOX 36
BOY 26
BOYFRIEND 148
BRAVE 216
BREAD 72
BREAK 93
BREAKFAST 83
breeze 17
BRIDGE 228
bright 19
BRIGHT 197

BRING 125
British 238
broad 228
brochure 137
BROKE 189
BROTHER 26
BROWN 36
BUG 216
BUILD 93
burden 112
BURN 135
business 180
BUSY 180
#BUSY 238
BUT 189
BUTTER 197
BUY 59
CALIFORNIA 101
call 62, 171
calm 137
camera 162
CAN 73, 111
CANADA 238
CANCEL 101
candidate 189
CANDY 94
CAN'T 111
capitol 170
CAPTION 189
capture 111
CAR 36
CAR-ACCIDENT 159
CAREFUL 169
CARELESS 169
carry 125
CAT 48
CATCH 111
CATHOLIC 238
CAUSE 207
caution 162
CELEBRATE 197
1-CENT 148
CENTER 228

CHAIR 37, 104
CHALLENGE 72
CHANGE 216
CHANNEL 228
chapter 49
charge 150
CHASE 159
CHAT 125
CHEAP 48
CHEESE 148
chemical 240
CHICAGO 125
chicken 180
CHILD 26
CHILDREN 94
CHINA 238
Chinese 238
CHOOSE 169
CHURCH 125
CITY 180
CLASS 37
CLEAN 48
CLEAN-UP 94
CLEAR 197
clever 19
close 127
CLOSE-DOOR 216
CLOTHES 72
COAT 83
COFFEE 72
COKE 72
COLD 48
COLLECT 111
COLLEGE 60
collide 159
collision 159
COLOR 37
COMB 101
COMB-HAIR 101
combine 229
COME 125
COME-ON 83
COMFORTABLE 197

TEMPLE 128	TRADE-PLACES-WITH 230	WAIT 75
TEMPT 230	train 39	WAKE-UP 139
TEND 192	TRAIN 102	WALK 63
terrible 48	transportation 161	WALK-TO 128
TEST 96	TRAVEL 200	WANT 39
THANK-YOU 39	TREE 105	WAR 230
THAT 128	TROPHY 172	WARM 19
THAT-ONE 128	TROUBLE 151	WARN 162
THEIR 28	TRUE 161	WASH 96
theirs 28	true 161	WASH-DISH 86
them 19	truth 217	WASH-FACE 96
THEMSELVES 96	TRY 115	WASHINGTON 63
then 60	TUESDAY 75	WASH-IN-MACHINE 96
THERE 128	TURKEY 162	WASTE 219
THEY 19	TURN-DOWN 210	WATCH 73
THIEF 172	TYPE 105	WATCH 73
THIN 172	TYPEWRITER 96, 105	WATER 63
THING 104	UGLY 19	way 138
THINK 115	UMBRELLA 75	WE 20
thirst 138	UNCLE 28	WEAK 20
THIRSTY 138	UNDERSTAND 51	weakness 20
THIS 128	unfortunate 48	wealthy 138
threat 207	university 60	WEAR 63
THROW-AWAY 151	UNTIL 86	wear 72
THURSDAY 75	UP 105	WEDDING 115
TICKET 75, 102	UPSTAIRS 210	WEDNESDAY 75
TIME 86	up to 86	1-WEEK 63
TIRED 19	URGE 128	week 63
TO-BICYCLE 105	us 20	WEIGH 210
TODAY 62	use 63	weird 151
together 151	used to 207	welcome 170
TOILET 93	USED-TO 62	WELL 51
TOMATO 240	usual 180	WEST 192
TOMORROW 62	VACATION 191	WET 139
TONIGHT 61	valuable 127	WHAT 96
TOTAL 182	value 148	WHAT-FOR 96
TO-TELEPHONE 62, 105	VERY 200	WHAT-TO-DO 96
TO-TTY 128	VISIT 63	WHAT'S-UP 96
TOUGH 209	vocabulary 51	WHEELCHAIR 192
tour 200	vocalize 138	WHEN 97
TOURNAMENT 192	VOICE 138	WHERE 97
town 180	volunteer 189	where 96
trade in 216	VOTE 219	WHICH 97

WHITE 39
WHITE PERSON 39
WHO 97
WHY 97
why 96
WIFE 28
WILL 63
WIN 115
WINDOW 103
WINE 151
WINTER 48
wish 49
WITH 151
WOMAN 28
WONDER 231

WONDERFUL 105
won't 114
WOOD 192
WORD 51
work out 159
WORK 51
WORLD 51
WORRY 97
WORSE 172
worth it 127
worth 148
WOW 105
WRENCH 162
WRIST-WATCH 75
write down 114

WRITE 63
WRONG 51, 192
YEAR 63
YELLOW 39
YES 51
YESTERDAY 63
YOU 20
YOUNG 51
YOU-PL 20
YOUR 29
YOUR-PL 29
yours 29
YOURSELF 97
YOURSELVES 97
youth 51